# 100 BEDTIME STORIES

**HAMLYN**
London · New York · Sydney · Toronto

**The stories in this book are by:**

W. H. Alexander Judith Banyard Jane Butterworth Sylvia Creche Gill Denton Mollie Donnelly Pamela Dormer Morley Dyer Joan Eadington Ivy Eastwick Iris Fox Judith Glover Janice Godfrey Jeanne Guy Tytus Huffman Valerie Anne Lloyd Eileen Mathias Gillian Maxwell M. W. McIntosh Isobel Milsome Daphne Peters Rosemary Pollitt Anne Robertson Myrtle Shaw Janet Slingsby Gordon Snell Margaret Torrington Jane Waller Freda Ward

**The illustrations are by:**

Glynnis Ambrus Rowan Barnes-Murphy David Barnett Shirley Bellwood Val Biro Lyn Burnes Corrine Burrows Alan Burton Brian Bysouth Ginny Chalcroft David Eaton Gwen Green Douglas Hall Susan Hunter Sandy Nightingale Stuart Perry Peter Richardson Caroline Sharpe Tony Streek

Cover illustration by Tony Streek

First published 1980 by The Hamlyn Publishing Group Limited
London · New York · Sydney · Toronto
Astronaut House, Feltham, Middlesex, England


ISBN 0 600 384 01 2 Printed in Italy

# Contents

# The grey feather

'It's a feather!' Joyce cried.

'But what kind of feather?' Tony asked.

The children looked down from the back door. By their mother's watering can lay a great grey feather.

'It's too big for any bird I know,' Tony said.

'There's another – and another!' Joyce cried. A line of feathers led from the back door across the lawn. The feathers ended in a clump of bushes.

'I love mysteries,' Joyce whispered to Tony. 'Let's see what's there.'

Tony picked up a broom for protection. 'Come on,' he said.

Cautiously the children followed the feathers. Near the bushes were smaller feathers.

'They're fluffy,' Joyce said. 'I'll just look into these bushes and . . .'

Slowly she parted the branches. There was a loud hiss. Joyce jumped back.

'A snake!' she cried. 'I saw its long neck!'

'I'll look,' Tony said. His voice trembled slightly. One hand held the broom firmly, the other parted the bushes.

Another loud hiss! Tony let go of the branches quickly.

'It's a great grey goose,' he whispered, 'sitting on a pile of feathers and fluff.'

'And it comes to the watering can for water,' Joyce smiled. 'Maybe it needs food, too.'

So each day the children placed food by the back door. And each day they watched as the goose came to eat and drink.

Then one morning the goose didn't appear. For two days it didn't come.

But the next morning the goose was back. Only this time she had a dozen yellow goslings with her.

# The Easter fair

In Tom's village every Easter a fair was held in the main street. Tom could see the roundabouts and swings, the coconut shies and the man selling candy floss from his bedroom window. You see, Tom and his parents lived above their sweet-shop in the main street, so Tom had an excellent view.

The shop closed at lunch-time when the fair got busy. Then Tom's mother was free to take him to visit the fair. Tom's favourite was the helter-skelter. While his mother watched, he climbed up and up and round and round until he reached the top of the tower. At the very top he sat on a mat and the man at the top of the helter-skelter gave him a little push. He came down round and round, faster and faster, too fast to see anything clearly until he reached the bottom where his mother was waiting to catch him.

Mummy bought him some candy floss. He loved seeing the man pour in the coloured crystals and the candy floss coming out looking just like a large piece of cotton wool on a stick.

At tea-time, the fair got busier. The children coming home from school came to enjoy the fun. Even the business men walking home from the station tried their hands at some of the stalls.

Tom was allowed to stay up late on the fair night. He watched from his bedroom window. It was really very noisy with the music playing loudly and excited screams from the people on the rides. When Tom grew sleepy, he said to his mother, 'I'll just get into bed and have a little rest. Then I'll watch again.' But he fell fast asleep.

The next morning, when he woke up, the fair had disappeared – every bit of it. There was no helter-skelter, no roundabout, no man selling candy floss. Only the road-sweepers cleaning the streets with their brooms and making everywhere tidy again.

Tom was sorry the fair had gone, but he knew it would come back again next year.

# Blue or green?

Daniel and Elizabeth watched their dad driving off to work one morning in his new car.

'Isn't it smart!' said Daniel. 'I *do* like Dad's new blue car.'

'It isn't blue!' said his sister, at once. 'It's green!'

The children argued and argued until, at last, Mum said, 'We'll talk to Dad as soon as he comes home again. If he says the car is green, then Elizabeth shall have a little prize for being right. If he says the car is blue, then Daniel shall have a little prize.'

The children waited eagerly for their dad to return and, at last, he arrived home for his tea.

While Dad was eating, Daniel said, 'Dad, our new car is definitely blue, isn't it?'

'No, it isn't, Dad – it's green, isn't it?' interrupted Elizabeth.

As soon as he had finished his meal, Dad brought out the little book that had come with the car.

'There!' said Dad. 'It says on this page – look – the official name of the colour of this model is *turquoise*.'

'Turquoise is a mixture of blue *and* green,' explained Mum. 'That means both of you were right, in a way.'

'But who has the little prize?' asked Daniel.

'You both do,' said Dad. 'The prize shall be a trip out into the country this evening. We'll go for a drive.'

# The naughty zebra

The children were happy because Grandad was taking them to the zoo. He bought a lollipop each for the children to enjoy as they walked around. Soon after that they came to the zebra enclosure.

Simon liked the zebras because their stripes reminded him of his pyjamas.

The children had a favourite zebra who always stood by the fence to greet visitors.

'Look, here's your zebra coming to see us,' said Grandad. 'I think she is getting to know you two.' Simon patted her head while Sarah licked her lollipop. Suddenly Sarah felt the zebra nibbling gently at her tee shirt. She turned round and before she knew what was happening the zebra put her head over the bar and knocked the lollipop out of her hand.

'You naughty zebra,' Sarah said and started to cry.

'I think it's the zebras' feeding time,' laughed Grandad.

Sarah dried her tears and went back to the shop to buy another lollipop, but this time she held it very tightly indeed!

# Paul the penguin

Paul was black-and-white, like all penguins, but he wasn't happy about it. He thought black-and-white was dull, and wanted to be in colour, like the parrot.

The parrot came from South America, and had bright red, green and blue feathers. It was always strutting about in its cage, showing them off.

One night, Paul scrambled over the fence round the penguin-pool, and began to walk with a sort of tiptoeing waddle, through the zoo.

He came to a shed, and pushed open the door. Inside, he found just what he was looking for: paint! There were tins and tins of it – red, blue, green, purple and yellow. Paul took the lids off all the tins, and then rushed from one to another, splashing paint over himself with his flippers, until there wasn't a patch of black or white to be seen on him. Happily, he wandered back along the path.

Paul slept well, and woke to the sound of . . . *laughter*! It was daylight, and the other penguins were standing around, pointing at him, and laughing loudly.

'What happened, Paul?' asked one. 'Did it rain paint, in the night?'

'We'll have to call you the Rainbow Penguin, now!' said another.

Paul didn't mind what they said. He was pleased to be so colourful. He didn't even mind the scornful squawks of the parrot.

Then he made an awful discovery: *he couldn't move*! The paint had dried, his flippers were stuck to his sides, and his feet were stuck together. When he tried to walk he just fell over.

The penguins laughed even more loudly. Then two of them came forward, picked him up, and threw him, with a big cheer, into the pool. They all jumped in after him, and began rubbing him with their flippers. Slowly, the paint came off, and Paul was his old black-and-white self again.

# Rosa Malairy

Rosa Malairy had one big wish. Her hair was long and black and hung in two thick plaits, but Rosa wished for blonde hair, golden as the sun, yellow as a sunflower.

When anyone said (and this often happened), 'Oh, Rosa, I wish my hair was long and black like yours,' Rosa would reply, 'It's horrid. Black hair is horrid.'

When someone else said, 'What lovely silky hair you have,' Rosa would reply, 'Do you think so? I don't.'

Then one day after school when she reached home, Rosa saw a huge bowl of yellow dye in the kitchen sink. Her mother had been dyeing white curtains yellow and was in the garden hanging them out to dry.

This was Rosa's great chance. She held her head down over the sink and then dipped it again and again into the bowl of yellow dye. 'Now,' she thought, 'I will have golden hair.' She grabbed a kitchen towel and rubber her hair dry.

When her mother came in from the garden and saw what Rosa had done, she nearly fainted. 'Oh my goodness! Oh my gracious! Rosa Malairy, what will you do next?' she said.

Rosa said, 'I've always wanted yellow hair, and now I've got yellow hair. Does it look nice?'

'It looks awful,' said her mother. 'I'll have to try to wash it out.' But, even as she spoke, she knew that it would be impossible. It was a very strong dye, excellent for making white curtains yellow, but not for hair.

'Go and look at yourself in the mirror,' Rosa's mother said and she spoke in a very faint whispery voice and closed her eyes as she spoke.

So Rosa went to her bedroom and looked in the mirror and when she saw her black and yellow streaky hair, much more of it yellow than black, she knew that she had made a bad, a very bad, mistake.

And next day she was sure that dyeing her pretty black hair yellow was worse than a mistake, for all her school-friends began calling after her, at the tops of their voices:

'Rosa Malairy
looks like a canary.'

# The toffee shop

Dame Treacle was a plump, jolly old lady who kept a toffee shop. People travelled from miles around to buy her delicious sweets.

One day a little boy came into the shop. 'Good morning,' smiled Dame Treacle. 'What can I do for you?'

The boy scowled. 'I want to open up my own toffee shop. Give me the recipe for your toffee,' he said crossly.

'It's a secret recipe,' said Dame Treacle. 'But you are welcome to try some. Here – have some of this.' She handed the boy a big piece of nut toffee.

The little boy snatched the toffee and took a huge bite. 'Groogh!' he said, pulling a face. 'It's horrible!'

'Dear me,' said Dame Treacle, 'no-one has ever complained before.'

The boy moaned and groaned and clutched his tummy. He staggered round the room howling. 'You wicked lady,' he wailed, 'your horrid toffee has given me tummy ache. Ooooh! How it hurts!'

'My goodness,' said Dame Treacle in alarm. She thought the boy was really ill, and ran out of the shop to fetch help.

A moment later, the little boy sat up and chuckled to himself. 'Ha!' he laughed. 'Now I can look for the secret recipe for this wonderful toffee.'

He went to the back of the shop and found a little yellow door leading to Dame Treacle's kitchen.

'It must be in here somewhere,' thought the boy. Then he saw a little box sitting on top of the highest shelf. He jumped up on to a stool and stretched out his hands. But he wasn't tall enough to reach the box. 'Bother! Bother! BOTHER!' shouted the boy. He jumped up as high as he could and grabbed the box. The stool wobbled and toppled over and the nasty little boy fell *plop* in to a big pot of treacle!

Dame Treacle returned with the village doctor. How they laughed to find the boy stuck in the treacle.

'You silly boy. The recipe is inside my head. No-one can steal it!' Dame Treacle said.

The boy was ashamed and said he was very sorry. So Dame Treacle forgave him and allowed him to help in the shop on busy days. And if you ever visit the toffee shop, you will find him always polite and helpful.

# Wacky the worm

One day Emma's dad said, 'Let's go for a walk in the park.'

So Emma and Emma's baby brother Charlie got ready. Emma put on her wellies to keep her feet dry and Charlie sat in the push-chair.

When they got to the park, Dad said, 'Shall we let Charlie have a little walk?'

'Yes,' said Emma.

So Dad lifted Charlie out of the push-chair and let him walk. Charlie was only little and he was just learning to walk. Sometimes he liked to crawl best. So guess what Charlie did? He didn't walk, he started to crawl. And he crawled away on to the wet grass.

'Come back!' said Emma, and she ran to fetch him. But when she got to him – guess what Charlie had found?

He had found a long, fat, wriggly, pink worm, and he was holding it tight.

Dad came and lifted Charlie up. 'You don't want a worm,' said Dad, 'worms live in the ground to help plants to grow.' But still Charlie clung to the worm.

'He likes it,' laughed Dad. 'We shall have to give it a name.'

'Let's call it Wacky,' said Emma. So they put Charlie back in his push-chair and took him home with Wacky the worm.

Then, guess what Emma did? She took Charlie to the window where there was a lovely red flower growing in a pot and they took Wacky the worm with them. And Charlie helped her to put Wacky in the soil, in the pot – to help the flowers to grow.

# Bill badger

Bill Badger poked his nose out of his hole in the sand-bank and sniffed cautiously.

The air was full of evening smells – wood-sorrel, dog's-mercury, damp moss and twigs. There were bird and animal smells too, drifting towards him in the warm air. Freddie Fox was about. He had a foxy smell, sharp and rough. Then Bill could smell pheasant, a feathery rich scent, and rabbit, a warm furry perfume.

These were all safe smells, so Bill Badger crept out of his hole, shook himself and rolled a little on the ground. Then he trotted off down the path.

Suddenly Bill Badger stopped short and froze with fear. There were two different dangerous smells. Peering through the leaves he saw . . . a dog connected to a man by a long lead. They were walking in the field close by.

Bill Badger crouched low and waited until they passed. Then the shadow of Owl passed over the pathway as he flew silently from the wood. 'Too-wit-too-woo' he said to Bill. 'The danger is passed now. Good evening to yoooooo.'

# Niblet the squirrel

Niblet was a squirrel who loved comfort. One day he wandered into Mick Mulberry's garage looking for somewhere cosy to sleep. He found it in the pocket of a paint-stained cardigan hanging on a nail. He curled his tail round his nose and went to sleep.

Niblet usually woke early, but a lot of late nights playing with his friends had made him tired, so he was still asleep when Mick came next morning to go to work.

Mick was a builder and carried his ladder to work on his van roof. He looked for a rag to tie on the back end of the ladder. This would warn other drivers not to come too close. He saw the cardigan, unhooked it, and tied it by the sleeves to the ladder.

At first Niblet slept on peacefully in the cardigan pocket, but, when he awoke, imagine his amazement to find himself dangling in space with cars on every side!

He climbed up the cardigan and clung to the ladder while drivers and school children leaned out of cars and buses to cheer.

At last they bumped through the gates of a building site. By then Niblet was once more dozing in the pocket. They stopped and Mick got out, put on his old cardigan and got his ladder off the van.

When Niblet woke up he thought he was in a tall tree. He peeped out. Not a leaf or branch was in sight, instead there were narrow plank platforms held up by a criss-cross of metal poles. The ground was a long way down because Mick was helping to put the roof on this new building. Niblet's nose twitched with excitement. Here was a wonderful adventure playground waiting for him to explore!

The workmen did very little building that morning. They all stopped to watch Niblet as he enjoyed showing off his wild acrobatics. He was just making his most daring jump when he landed, plop, in a bucket of cement. Luckily, Mick grabbed him and rinsed him in a bucket of water.

From then on Niblet often travelled with Mick when he went to work.

Niblet had many more adventures on many more building-sites, but he never showed off quite so much again!

# George's new house

One morning, George woke up feeling very glum. He gave a big stretch, climbed out of his wicker basket, and wondered why he felt so miserable. Then he remembered. He'd moved house!

George was a town dog. He was small, and black and white, with one brown and one black ear. And until yesterday he'd been very happy with life because he and his family had lived in town.

Outside the house there were lamp posts to sniff and lots of other dogs to bark at, and sometimes Emma and Mummy would take George to the recreation ground and let him off the lead, and he'd run very fast. George had been very happy with his life.

But yesterday a big van had arrived and men had got out and started picking up his family's furniture and putting it in the big van. George had been very worried – he'd even growled when one of the men had picked up HIS basket.

'Don't be silly, George,' Emma had said. 'You'll get your basket back when we arrive at the new house in the country.'

New house! Country! It made George miserable just to think about it. He liked the town. He didn't want to move. He didn't know anything about the country and although he couldn't see much when he arrived there with the family because it was dark, he didn't think he'd like it.

The next morning he sat in his basket and howled.

'Come on, old boy,' said Daddy. 'We're going to the woods!' George cocked his ears and wagged his tail while Daddy put his collar and lead on. He didn't actually know what woods were because he was a town dog but anything was better than sitting here feeling miserable.

Emma, Daddy and George walked down the road past half a dozen houses and two barking dogs. George felt happier. 'Perhaps I'll come and visit here this afternoon,' he thought, and barked a greeting to them.

Eventually they reached a lot of trees – more trees than George had ever seen in his life. He raced through the woods, barking and wagging his tail. He chased dozens of rabbits and brought lots of sticks for Daddy to throw.

On the way home one of the dogs he'd passed earlier ran out barking and growling. George barked and growled back.

'Somebody to have fights with!' thought George happily.

When he got home he sat and looked at the garden. A very large garden. Plenty of places to bury bones. Plenty of room to run. He settled down for a snooze in the sun.

'I think I like being a country dog,' he thought sleepily.

# The baby seal

'Come back!' called Mummy Seal, but the baby seal didn't hear. The baby seal didn't *want* to hear. He was having far too much fun! He was chasing such a splendid fish.

On he swam, rushing through the deep sea. Then suddenly the sea narrowed into a river, and Baby Seal became excited. 'I shall catch the fish here,' he thought. 'I'm sure to catch it where the river ends!' And he tried harder, the tide carrying him in as he swam. Soon, the river narrowed to a creek, with boats tied up at either side.

He began to feel a little nervous, swimming underneath the keels of the boats. Then, BAM! He was up against a huge, wooden door. It was the lock gates and he could swim no further. Where was his fish?

It wasn't anywhere to be seen. And with a horrible, sick feeling, the baby seal realised he was lost, miles away from home. He swam around the boats unhappily.

'Oh why,' he thought sadly, 'didn't I listen to Mummy? I should have stopped when she called,' and he sobbed to himself under the water.

Then he remembered Mummy telling him about men, and a shiver ran down his back. 'Beware always of men,' she had said, 'for some men are seal catchers, and will kill you for your fur.'

Baby Seal shuddered. Were there seal catchers here? He raised his head above the water to see. And the boat at the side of him rocked, as a man stepped into it.

Before he knew what was happening, the man had reached over the side and caught him. He struggled frantically, but with a lift of strong arms, he was dragged into the boat. He was caught! He was caught!

Fisherman Bob stroked him gently as he spoke. 'Now, now, little chap, don't be frightened, I won't hurt you. It's lucky that I found you for I'm just going fishing, and can take you back to the sea.'

And that's just what he did. Fisherman Bob gave the baby seal a lift in his boat back to the sea, and there he found Mummy Seal again. He doesn't ever disobey her, now.

# The jade elephant

Hannah's father travelled a good deal for his work. Neither Hannah nor her mother liked him going away, but each time he came home he brought Hannah a small present from the country he'd just visited.

From Russia he had brought back a painted wooden doll that came apart in the middle. Inside was a smaller doll and inside that doll an even smaller one. In all there were about six dolls, and the last was the tiniest of all.

From France, Daddy brought her a doll dressed in traditional costume.

From Sweden came a small wooden horse. He was hand carved and painted red with flowers on his back.

One day Daddy told Hannah and her mother that he was going to China. 'Goodness,' said Hannah, 'is that far away?'

'Yes,' said Daddy, 'it's a very long way from home.'

He found the atlas and showed Hannah just where China was. 'What will you bring me back from China, Daddy?' asked Hannah.

'Well,' said Daddy, 'you shouldn't ask, but perhaps it might be a piece of jade.'

Lucy thought that sounded rather dull but she didn't hurt her daddy's feelings by saying so.

Daddy was away some weeks, but at last Hannah's mother received a telegram saying that he would be back in three days' time.

How slowly those three days seemed to go. But at last it was time to go to the airport to meet him. Hannah knew better this time than to ask her father what he had brought her as a present. But when they reached home Daddy gave Hannah another hug and said, 'You've been a very patient little girl and here's your reward.'

From his pocket he took a small box. When Hannah took off the lid there was only a piece of cotton wool. But under that was something small and green. It was a tiny green elephant with a little gold loop on his back through which was threaded a fine gold chain.

'Do you like it?' asked Daddy. 'I thought you were old enough now to have a necklace of your own. Jade from China is something very special, the Chinese call it their jewel of heaven.'

'I think it's very special too,' said Hannah. She often wore the little elephant round her neck and it always reminded her of the time her daddy returned from China.

# Mr Stray

Mr Stray was an old, battered, wheezy stray cat.

Timothy heard him meowing outside the front door one cold rainy day. When he opened it, in walked the old cat.

'That's a real wandering cat, I can tell,' Timothy's father said. 'He won't stay long so let's call him Mr Stray.'

'Yes, give Mr Stray a bowl of milk,' Timothy's mother suggested, 'and then he'll probably wander away again.'

But how wrong they all were! First Mr Stray slept all that day in front of the fire. Then he slept all that night in front of the fire. When he awoke he stretched, yawned and just lay in front of the fire until his next meal.

On and on this went with Mr Stray getting so fat and well-fed, so sleek and so chubby and round they soon had to think of another name for him.

Mother suggested Fatty. Father said they could call him Chubby. But Timothy's name was best.

'Mr Stay!' he said, 'let's call him Mr Stay, because he just stays and stays and stays!'

In fact Mr Stay is staying there still for all we know.

# Cathy's plant

Cathy loved Grandad's greenhouse. It was another world in there, all warm and moist. There were plants in pots, plants in boxes, tiny plants and large plants.

One day Grandad said to her, 'Would you like to take a small plant home, and grow it yourself?'

'Oh thank you!' said Cathy. 'Will it have beautiful flowers like yours?'

'Yes,' said Grandad. 'Bring it to show me, when it does!'

At home, Cathy put her plant on a window-sill. There, she looked after it and watered it.

A few days later, she noticed *two* little plants in her pot. And one was growing faster than the other. She remembered what Grandad had told her – never have two plants in one pot. So she pulled the smaller one out.

The little plant that was left grew well under Cathy's care, and became quite large.

She waited hopefully for a flower-bud, but none came.

Then Mummy said, 'I'm sure that plant is not the same as the ones Grandad is growing.' Cathy felt quite worried.

'Bring it to show me,' said Grandad, when they told him. So they wrapped it carefully, and took it to his greenhouse.

When Grandad saw it, he laughed loudly. 'Oh Cathy!' he laughed, 'has it stung you?'

'Stung me?' echoed Cathy, and Mummy stared.

'Yes,' said Grandad. 'What you've grown here is – a nettle!'

'Oh dear!' said Cathy. 'I must have pulled out the wrong seedling!'

# The Christmas tree

It was Christmas Eve. Everyone felt excited, especially the little Christmas tree standing on the window-sill looking out into the garden. Its branches glittered with tinsel, golden bells and silver stars, and when darkness fell each evening its coloured lights were switched on. Then it felt like a magic tree! 'How beautiful!' said all the people walking by.

In the front garden stood another Christmas tree. Once, some years before, it had held out its branches to be hung with sparkling lights and gleaming bells. But now it was forgotten. It sighed and sadly shed a few of its needle-like leaves on the ground.

But somebody cared about the sad little Christmas tree. Almost too small to be seen, something stirred on its top-most tip. Much too lightly to be heard, it dropped to the first small branch and hurried along it. Then it swung down to the next branch, and down and down and down. Reaching the ground it climbed up and began all over again.

A clock struck . . . ten, eleven, twelve. It was Christmas Day! The moon shone right down into the front garden and lit up the little Christmas tree. It was hung all over with diamonds and pearls, strung on threads of silver gossamer!

'Who have I to thank for this?' asked the Christmas tree wonderingly, looking at the webs of silver lace spun between its branches.

The tree in the window stared out between the curtains in amazement. 'Whoever would bother to decorate a tree in a garden?' it asked. But nobody answered. The tiny decorator of the garden Christmas tree swung gleefully from its top-most tip, spinning on a silver thread with its eight legs neatly folded.

As for the tree in the window, a week after Christmas it

was stripped of all its tinsel and bells which were packed into a cardboard box. You may wonder if the tree was planted in the garden like the other one. It was not. It was folded up and laid on a shelf in a cupboard, for it was made of wire and plastic.

'*You* needn't wait till next Christmas to sparkle again,' whispered the tiny decorator to the real tree. And many mornings the early sunbeams danced on the dew-drops hanging on the threads the spider had spun.

# Sheila's sandcastle

Sheila loved going to the sea-side and, most of all, she loved building sandcastles. On the first day of her holiday she ran along the beach with her spade and her orange bucket, looking for a good spot to build a castle. She found a place not too near the water, but not too far away, either – so that the sand was just right, not too wet, and not too dry.

Then she started building, filling the bucket again and again with sand, and tipping it upside down, to make a nice, round tower, each time. She always made one tower for the middle, then a circle of towers around it, then another circle outside that. Then she dug a shallow ditch all around.

When she was just starting the second circle, her Uncle Barry walked over and looked at what she had done.

'That's very good, Sheila,' he said. 'Can I help you?'

'Oh yes, Uncle Barry,' said Sheila.

Uncle Barry knelt down beside her, but instead of going on with the circle of towers, he started to build a wall. Then he made a hole through the wall, and said, 'Look! A door-way!' It wasn't the kind of castle Sheila had planned.

Then, her father came up, and asked, 'Can *I* join in?'

'Oh yes, Daddy,' said Sheila.

'I think I'll do some decorating,' said her father, and he began fetching shells and sticks and bits of sea-weed, and

putting them on top of the towers and the wall. They looked nice – but it wasn't the kind of castle Sheila had planned.

'Hey, that's quite a castle!' said her cousin, Martin. 'Can I help?'

But before Sheila could say anything, her uncle said, 'Yes yes, of course, Martin – the more, the merrier!'

Then Martin shouted across to Sheila's big sister, Maria, 'Come on, Maria – we're helping Sheila build her sandcastle!'

Maria came over, and said, '*I* know! I'll dig a channel down to the sea, so the water will come up and lap around the castle.'

Sheila was going to say that she didn't *want* the water lapping around the castle, but Maria was already digging, and the others were far too busy to notice Sheila.

Half an hour later, they all stood up and watched the water coming up the channel and lapping around the castle.

'What a splendid castle!' said Uncle Barry. 'I think we've all done a wonderful job, don't *you*, Sheila?'

There was no answer. They looked around. A few yards further up the beach Sheila was busy on her own, with her bucket and spade, building the castle *she* wanted to build: the one with a tower in the middle, and a circle of towers round it, and another circle round that, and then a ditch . . .

# The red socks

The Threadgold family had been invited to their cousin's wedding. Johnathan, who was the youngest member of the family, immediately decided that he wanted to wear his new red socks for the occasion because they were his favourite pair.

'You can't wear red socks,' his sister Judith exclaimed. 'Not to a posh wedding. You'll look like a footballer.'

'He's not wearing his red socks,' Mother said sternly. 'He'll wear what I say he'll wear and that's that!'

'What colour can I wear then?' Johnathan mumbled under his breath.

'White,' said his father.

'*White*?' shouted Johnathan. 'White isn't a colour. I hate white, my legs are white, in fact all of me is white and, besides, Judith always wears white socks and I don't want to wear the same as her . . . I don't want to.'

'That's enough, thank you Johnathan,' said his mother firmly.

Johnathan didn't mention the matter again until a few

days before the wedding when he managed to persuade Judith to agree to smuggle out his favourite red socks under her hat!

The big day arrived and Johnathan happily went to the church in his white socks.

While the choir and congregation sang, Johnathan quietly removed one white sock, and then another white sock and stuffed them behind a radiator!

Getting the red socks out from under Judith's hat was a bit more difficult, but they managed it and when everyone got down to pray Johnathan popped them on. PHEW!

With their heads in the air and staring straight ahead the children followed the congregation, who followed the bride and groom, into the sunshine outside.

'Johnathan!' It was his mother's voice. 'How *could* you! After all I said. Where are your proper wedding socks? Where . . .' She stopped as the photographer pointed his camera at them all.

'Smile everybody, please,' shouted the photographer. Just at that moment the bridegroom yelled 'SNAP!', lifted up the legs of his trousers and exposed a pair of the brightest red socks you have ever seen.

What a picture!

# The barn owls

The barn owls had lived for many years in a barn on the edge of a village. Two little owlets blinked up at their parents from the pile of feathers and bones that was their nest. Soon it would be dark and the adult barn owls would have to go out and hunt for food.

The barn owls glided silently over the sleeping countryside. They both had very good hearing and the slightest sound in the undergrowth would mean the end of a mouse, or some other small creature which owls like to eat. It was almost dawn when they arrived back at the barn. The little owlets were waiting noisily; they were very hungry. When the owlets had eaten enough the barn owls settled down to sleep.

They had been asleep for only a little while when they were suddenly woken up by a banging and shouting outside the barn. The barn owls flew silently to an opening in the barn roof and looked out. A strange sight met their eyes. Outside were strange, brightly coloured machines and men

hammering poles into the ground.

The barn owls did not understand what was happening but they knew that it meant danger to their young. They would have to move the owlets, but where to? And when? It was dangerous to go out when the men were about. They would wait for an opportunity when the men went to sleep.

As darkness fell it grew silent and the owls set off on their search. Their new home needed to be far away from the danger that threatened them but near enough for them to carry their young. They had been flying for perhaps five minutes when they spotted an empty farmhouse. There was a hole in the roof just the right size for them to squeeze through. This was a safe place to make their new home.

They flew swiftly back to the barn and carefully made the journey from the old home to the new with first one owlet and then the other, the mother owl carrying them carefully in her beak.

The barn owls sat in the hole in the roof and watched the first rays of sunshine creep over the countryside. They were very happy. They had saved their babies and found a new home.

# Georgina

Sally had been given a cat for her birthday. Mother had told her it was a male cat so Sally called it George.

George soon grew into a very big fat cat who was quite content to sit on the windowsill and watch the world go by.

'There's something wrong with that cat,' Mother said.

'No there isn't, Mummy,' Sally told her. 'He just likes to sit and think.'

A few days later when Sally got home from nursery school she found that George was not in his usual 'thinking' position on the windowsill. She and her mother searched the whole house but there was no sign of dearest George.

By the time Sally's father arrived home they were both upset. There was still no sign of George.

'Tea!' Sally's father suggested to cheer them up. 'I'll go and put the kettle on.' They heard him say, 'This stupid washing machine's stopped working. The door's open.' Then he yelled, 'Come quickly.'

Sally and Mummy ran into the kitchen and there, sitting inside the drum of the washing machine, was George with three tiny kittens!

'George is a father!' shouted Sally. Then again, 'I mean George is a mother! George was a Georgina all the time!'

# Magnus mouse

Magnus was a little white mouse who belonged to a boy named Danny. He was a very tame little mouse, and Danny often let him out of his cage so that he could run about on the bedroom floor.

One afternoon, when they were playing together, Danny's mother called him downstairs to eat his tea. 'You needn't go back into your cage,' Danny told Magnus. 'Stay here, I won't be long.' And he gave Magnus a piece of cheese to nibble at.

Danny ate his tea quickly. But when he went back up to his bedroom, he couldn't see Magnus anywhere! Where had he gone?

Suddenly, Danny heard a peculiar noise. 'Plink-plonk,' it went. 'Plink-plink-plonk.'

'That's strange,' thought Danny. There it was again – 'plonk-plink.' It sounded just like his toy piano!

Quietly, Danny crept across the bedroom to the toy cupboard. The door was open just a crack, and he peeped inside. And there – was Magnus! He was running up and down the piano keys and having a wonderful time.

# The moorhens

The sun was just rising above the farmer's fields. The cock in the chicken shed began to crow. In the big pond at the bottom of the farm a moorhen swam quietly out from among the tall reeds. Her black and white tail flicked back and forth. Her red eyes looked around. There was no-one about.

She gave a croak and two baby moorhens swam out of the reeds. They were black and fluffy.

The mother dived under the water. The chicks tried to follow. They ducked their heads and paddled. But they were too light to go under. They just swam along with their tails in the air.

The mother rose to the surface a few yards ahead. The family climbed on to the shore and began to nibble the weeds and grass there.

Slowly they grazed farther and farther from the pond. Now they were on the edge of the farmer's lawn. On one side was his house, on the other his vegetable garden.

Carefully, cautiously, the mother led her family across the open lawn. Her one eye was on the house, the other on the vegetable patch.

When they reached the garden the mother went first to the lettuce. She tore off the outer leaves and ate them. The chicks ate the soft centres.

Then the moorhen went to the cabbages. They were tightly-packed but the mother jabbed her beak through the hard outer leaves. The chicks stuck their bills into the holes and ate and ate.

Suddenly there was a startled cry from above. 'Out of my garden, you pests!' the farmer shouted. He had come out to weed his garden. Swinging his hoe he came at the moorhens.

The little family scattered. They ran across the lawn, their necks outstretched, their bodies bent forward. The farmer ran right behind them waving his hoe.

When the birds reached the pond the mother dived under the water. And this time, paddling furiously, the chicks did too.

When the chicks came out of the water they were in the centre of the reeds. Their mother was already in the nest. They crawled in under her.

Night fell. Now it was the end of the day. In the trees around the pond an owl hooted. In the distance a fox barked.

And in the farmhouse the farmer made plans to fence in his garden the next day.

# Puss and Boo-Hoo

Puss was a deaf old cat. He spent each day asleep in the front window of a little antique shop.

Ali Kasem Ring-a-Djinn-Djinn was a genie, a magical being who lived in a blue-green bottle.

One morning Ali Kasem's blue-green bottle was placed in the front window of the antique shop where Puss lived. Now the rule that a genie lives by is this: whenever anyone rubs his bottle the genie must pop out. Then the genie says, 'I am your slave, O master of the bottle. I can grant you any wish. Just speak, O master. I obey.' Then whoever rubs the bottle makes a wish – any wish he wants.

Now back to the front window in the antique shop early one morning.

The sun was just rising as the cat crawled through the back curtains. He stretched and yawned, tired from a night's

work hunting. Then he walked over to the blue-green bottle. It was warm from the sun. The cat circled around it. As he did so he rubbed his back against the bottle. Then he curled up at its base and fell asleep.

The genie awoke inside. 'Hooray!' he cheered. 'Someone rubbed my bottle. Someone wants to make a wish!'

Out of the bottle he poured. A blue-green cloud of him filled the front window. Two red eyes looked around. Then the genie saw the cat curled around the bottle. 'Your wish is my command, O master,' he spoke in a voice of thunder.

The cat didn't answer.

'I am the slave of the bottle, O four-footed one,' the genie rumbled again. 'I can grant your slightest wish. Just command and it is done.'

The cat purred on.

'Hey, pussy cat!' the genie cried, despair in his voice. 'Didn't you rub? Don't you want something? Nice mouse? Hot milk? Tin of cat food?' His voice went higher and higher ending in a sob.

But the cat just purred quietly on and on.

The genie looked sad. Big purple circles appeared under his eyes. A tear trickled down his nose. He sniffed, then he popped back into his bottle.

The next morning it happened again. Over the days, over the weeks, over the months – the same routine! In came the cat. Rub, rub on the bottle. Out popped the genie. 'Purr, purr,' went the cat. Back into the bottle popped the genie with a sob.

Pop out! Pop in! Pop out! Pop in! Every day! Seven times a week! Thirty times a month! Three hundred and sixty-five times a year! Until all Ali Kasem Ring-a-Djinn-Djinn could cry was 'Boo-hoo, boo-hoo.'

This went on for so long that in the world of fellow genies Ali Kasem's real name was forgotten. And he was forever after known as Boo-Hoo the Popper.

# Toothpaste!

Isobel had been sent to her room *again* for 'icing' the wash basin with the toothpaste.

'Why do you keep on doing it?' her mother asked. 'Every morning and evening I find toothpaste crinkled all round the wash basin, over the taps, round the soap, but never on your toothbrush where it's supposed to be!'

'But it's such good fun,' insisted Isobel, 'it just oozes out and lets me make shapes.'

The next morning Isobel went into the bathroom and remembered not to play with the toothpaste. But at bedtime, she made a 'rosebud' on each tap and two 'eyes' on the soap.

Mother was so angry this time that she just put Isobel to bed without saying one word. Then she went downstairs to finish baking her cake.

The following afternoon Isobel asked if she could please have a piece of her mother's cake for her tea.

'Of course, Isobel,' said mother cutting her a slice. Isobel sank her little white teeth into the soft white icing.

Then suddenly she let out a yell. 'It's TOOTHPASTE!'

'And "iced" especially for you,' grinned Mother. 'That should remind you never to treat toothpaste like icing again!'

# Henry the parrot

Henry lived on a wooden perch in the back room of an old junk shop. Mr Murdoch, who owned the shop, was a miserable, grumpy old man who never spoke to Henry. In fact he never spoke much to anyone. The only words that Henry heard him say often were, 'Don't touch that!' which he shouted a dozen times a day at his unfortunate customers.

Every Tuesday, Henry was left alone on his perch while Mr Murdoch went out buying more junk. Henry usually had a sleep on Tuesdays as there was nothing to do.

He was in the middle of a dream in which he turned into an eagle and carried off Mr Murdoch, when he heard strange voices in the shop. Peering round on his perch he saw two men helping themselves to various bits of junk.

How *dare* they! 'Don't touch that,' Henry squawked flying off his perch and straight for the thieves. 'Don't touch that!'

Scared out of their wits the burglars dropped the bags and ran for their getaway car. They drove off in such a hurry that they crashed into a police car and were caught.

The policemen were so impressed with Henry, that they asked Mr Murdoch if they could buy him and keep him as their lucky mascot.

Now Henry lives at the police station and has lots of fun talking to all the policemen.

# Tommy Tadpole

Tommy Tadpole was discontented. Ever since he had swum to the top of the pond, and had seen the bright colours of the world above the water, he had hated his black coat. How he longed for a coat of brilliant yellow like the kingcups, freckled with green, the colour of the water-lily leaves.

Everyone in the pond was tired of Tommy's grumbles, and they pretended to be busy whenever he swam by. His crowds of brothers and sisters darted off into the weed when he started to talk about green and yellow coats. The water snails stayed in their shells, the water beetles crawled away, and the minnows just laughed, shooting past in a silvery shoal. His only friend was a caddis larva, an ugly little fellow in a mosaic vest made of tiny stones.

'It must be dull living at the bottom of the pond,' said Tommy. 'I'd be bored if I were you.'

'Well, you're not me!' said the caddis larva. 'Anyway, one day I shall grow wings and fly away.'

'I don't believe it,' said Tommy, and he laughed even louder than the minnows.

One day he saw the caddis larva climbing slowly up a plant stem.

'It won't be long now,' said the larva cheerfully.

'What won't be long now?' asked Tommy.

'The day when I get my wings and fly away,' he answered. Tommy laughed and turned three quick somersaults.

Next day the caddis larva had climbed half out of the water. Tommy pushed his head out of the water to see what was happening. He was just in time, for the larva had wriggled out of its vest, and now it sat drying a pair of beautiful gossamer wings.

'Is it really you?' asked Tommy in amazement.

'Your turn next,' called the caddis fly as he flew away. Tommy leapt after him, but frogs can't fly and he landed on another lily leaf. He looked at his reflection. It was magnificent!

'I suppose I was so busy grumbling that I never noticed my legs growing and my tail disappearing!' he said to himself.

'I'm a frog!' he told the world in a jubilant croak. 'And your coat is a beautiful green and yellow,' sang the willows.

# The steamroller

Back and forth went the steamroller. 'Chugga, chugga,' he said as he went over the stones that he'd squashed quite flat, and over some more straight after that.

'Ting-a-ling,' rang a bicycle bell. 'What are you doing, steamroller?'

'Making a road for you to ride on,' answered the steamroller.

'Thank you,' tinkled the bell on the bicycle.

'Thank you,' tooted a motor car on the other side of the road.

Then the car and the bicycle went on their way and the steamroller went on with his work. All that week the

steamroller worked hard running over the stones.

On Sunday the bicycle came along but the steamroller wasn't there. He was in a gateway at the side of the road. The motor car also came to look.

'Toot, toot,' he said, 'this is a lovely road to ride on.'

'Ting-a-ling,' tinkled the bell, 'yes, a lovely road for us to glide on.'

The steamroller heard them and smiled happily for he too was pleased with his week's work. 'Chugga, chugga,' he said.

# Chloe

Chloe the guinea pig went to live with Alison, Bridget and Neil in a cottage by the sea. Chloe was beautiful, she had long pale brown hair which the children's mummy combed every day with a special pink comb, kept only for combing Chloe's hair.

At night Chloe had her own little cage in the garage, where she slept nice and safe and snug.

Every morning Bridget brought Chloe her breakfast, fresh green lettuce and carrots. She would leave the cage door open so Chloe was free to spend the day exploring the garden.

Chloe loved the garden. It was all gold and green in the morning and the grass was dewy fresh. The flowers were blue and pink, orange and purple, all holding their petal faces up to the sun.

One day when Chloe was let into the garden, she was feeling very naughty. 'I'm going into the vegetable patch,' she said. 'I know I'm not allowed in there but I do want to go in just to have a look.'

So off she went, and the first thing she saw were the green runner bean plants and their bright red flowers – and do you know what she did? She started to count one, two, three, four, five and she went snip, snip, snip, snip, snip with her sharp white teeth, and she had bitten through all five plants. 'Oh dear,' said Chloe, 'I didn't mean to bite through them, but they did look so nice and tasty.'

Poor little Chloe, she was so upset about what she had done she hadn't noticed where she was going, and when she looked about her she was in a strange garden, where the grass was tall and thick. Two large tears trickled down Chloe's face. What was she to do, how was she going to get home again?

Suddenly – two large friendly hands picked her up and stroked her gently, 'So this is where you have been, I've been looking all over for you, come and have your hair combed.'

Chloe was so happy she was safe again. The children's mummy had found her and she was going to have her hair combed. She decided that she was going to try very hard from now on to do just as she was told.

# Twenty-two frogs

'Mummy, Mummy, come and look,' shouted Martin excitedly as he raced into the kitchen, 'our tadpoles have grown tiny legs.'

'My, they are growing quickly, Martin,' said Mummy. 'Soon we must take them back to the pond where you and Wendy found them. We can't have twenty-two frogs hopping around the house.'

'Oh, why can't we keep them?' asked Martin. 'Then we would have lots of pets.'

'No, darling,' said Mummy kindly, 'we can't have all those frogs hopping and jumping around the house. They wouldn't like it, either. They like to live near ponds and streams where there is lots of water for them to swim. Frogs don't like living in the town.'

'Couldn't we fill the bath and let them swim in that sometimes?' asked Martin.

Mummy laughed. 'No, Martin. In a few days we must take the baby frogs back to the pond where they came from.'

On the day the baby frogs had to be taken back to the pond, Martin felt rather sad. He liked them at home and didn't want to take them back.

Suddenly there was a loud shriek from the bathroom.

'Martin!' Mummy shouted, and she rushed down the stairs. 'Did you put these two frogs in the bath? You naughty boy! You knew we must take them back today.'

Martin grinned, 'I'm sorry Mummy, I didn't mean to frighten you. I just thought I could keep those three frogs at home.'

'Three frogs? There aren't three frogs, there are only two,' said Mummy. 'Where has the other one gone?'

Mummy, Daddy and Martin searched everywhere for the other frog but could not find it.

Then Martin looked out of the window. There, outside, he saw the tiny frog hopping across the road.

'Daddy! Daddy!' Martin shouted. Daddy ran into the room and Martin pointed but, as he did, a huge lorry came rumbling down the road towards the frog.

Martin just closed his eyes and cried. 'If I had left them in the tank, none of this would have happened,' he sobbed.

'It's all right Martin,' Daddy said, as the lorry passed their house. 'The frog has hopped out of the way again. I must run out and get it quickly.'

Daddy carried the bouncy little frog back to Martin. Martin still had big tears rolling down his cheeks. 'Let's take them all back to the pond, Daddy. Mummy was right, they will be happier there. The town is much too dangerous for tiny frogs.'

# Grandpa's goat

Granny asked Michael and Mandy to help her carry some boxes to the Jumble Sale. She was taking a lot of old clothes to be sold there.

'It's a very warm morning,' said Granny, taking off her flowered straw hat and putting it down on the heap of jumble clothes. 'I've asked Grandpa to take the goat for a walk in the sunshine, while we're out.'

The children loved their grandpa's goat. It was friendly, and would eat *anything*.

Granny and the children carried the old clothes into the Jumble Sale. There were so many clothes that they kept sliding on to the ground, and in all the muddle Granny forgot that her straw hat was amongst them.

Michael bought a trumpet and some old records, and Mandy bought some clothes for dressing up – a sparkly frock and some shoes with high heels.

Then Granny remembered her straw hat.

'Oh dear, I hope no-one's sold it,' she said, looking round anxiously.

But the first thing she saw was Grandpa's goat!

'The goat has taken Grandpa for a walk – to find us!' said Michael in delight.

Suddenly the goat slipped its lead out of Grandpa's hand, and there was confusion everywhere as the goat became very excited and butted at one of the tables, which tipped right over. Everything slid to the floor and the goat found itself entangled in a long woolly scarf and a string of beads. Then it started eating a hat.

'That's my straw hat!' cried Granny.

'He's eating it,' giggled Mandy. Somehow Grandpa managed to catch the goat by bending down and grabbing it from underneath a pile of jumpers.

As he did so, a brooch fell to the ground. It was pretty, and Grandpa bought it for Granny as a surprise.

'Why, that's lovely,' smiled Granny. 'It quite makes up for having my hat eaten.'

They made a very funny procession going home. Michael led the way carrying his pile of records and blowing the trumpet. He was followed by Mandy in her sparkly frock and high-heeled shoes.

Then came Granny, looking slightly flustered but smart in her twinkling new brooch.

Finally, Grandpa and the goat came along. The goat still had the scarf and the string of beads draped round its horns, while it chewed the last mouthfuls of hat.

# Behind the clouds

Sue and Andy were very lucky. Their parents were taking them on holiday to Spain, and they were going to fly there in an aeroplane.

As they drove to the airport, Sue and Andy got more and more excited. They had never been in an aeroplane. Mummy and Daddy were excited too. It was cold and raining and they were looking forward to lots of warm sunshine in Spain.

They left their car in a huge multi-storey car park, and walked over to the airport buildings. Mummy and Daddy gave in their cases to a man behind a desk, and then they hurried down a long corridor and out through some swing doors. There was a bus waiting. 'Hurry up and get on,' said Mummy.

'What!' shouted Andy, 'You said we were going on an aeroplane.' He was very upset.

Daddy laughed, 'Shhh,' he said. 'It's all right. This bus is going to take us to the aeroplane.'

Sue kicked Andy. 'You are silly,' she said.

'You didn't know we had to go on a bus either,' Andy said crossly.

'Never mind,' said Mummy, 'climb inside and we'll soon be at the plane.'

The bus didn't go very far. It stopped under the wings of an enormous aeroplane. Everyone hurried out and climbed the steps into the plane.

The engines roared and the plane began to move down the runway. Suddenly it was up in the air and the buildings on the ground began to look smaller and smaller.

Then, all at once, everything vanished. All there was outside the windows was a thick, white blanket of what looked like fog. Sue was quite scared. 'What's happened?' she cried.

'It's clouds,' said Daddy. 'You remember how it was cold and raining on the ground? Well, here are the clouds we saw in the sky. We are inside them now.'

The children were rather disappointed. They wanted to look down at all the tiny things on the ground. 'Wait a minute,' said Mummy, 'I think something exciting will happen.'

Sue and Andy waited, then suddenly the aeroplane shot out of the clouds into a blue, blue sky.

They looked out and saw a thick layer of white clouds beneath them, but blue sky above with the sun shining brightly, just like on the hottest summer's day at home.

'The sun is always shining during the day time,' explained Mummy, 'but often clouds get in the way and stop us seeing it. Now we are behind the clouds.'

'Let's hope the clouds go before we reach Spain,' Daddy said, 'so that we can see the sun while we are on the ground!'

Very soon the clouds did disappear, and Sue and Andy looked down. They saw the sea far below, and later on they saw mountains. They enjoyed it all so much that they were sorry when it was time for the plane to land.

# The snow-creature

One winter morning, a little girl named Lucy woke up to find that everywhere was covered with snow.

'Are you going to build a snowman in the garden?' her mother asked her.

Lucy thought for a moment – and then she had a wonderful idea. 'Not a snow*man*,' she said. 'I think I'll build something different.'

First she made a round snowball, and then she began to roll the snowball through the snow. As it rolled along, it grew bigger and bigger, and heavier and heavier, until Lucy couldn't roll it any further.

'That's the body,' she told herself. Then she made another snowball, but this one was smaller than the first. 'And that's the head,' she told herself.

Then she added two round snow-ears, and a big round snow-nose, and two shiny black pebbles for the eyes, and a thin twig for the mouth. And lastly, she scraped away some of the snow to give the snow-creature two fat paws.

There – it was finished! Lucy was very pleased that her idea had worked so well, and she called her mother to come and see.

What a surprise her mother had! Because do you know what Lucy had built? It wasn't a snow*man*. It was a snow-*bear*!

# Harry's puppies

Harry wanted a pet, so he made up a 'pretend' puppy, called Joe. Joe was brown, with floppy ears, and he went everywhere with Harry.

At meals, Joe sat on the table beside Harry's plate. When Harry was in the bath, Joe swam round and round in the water, with the yellow duck and the little red ship. When Harry went to bed, Joe lay there beside him.

For his next birthday, Harry was given a *real* puppy. It was black and white, with a waggy tail, and was called Jake. Harry loved Jake, and wanted to take him everywhere, just like Joe. But when he tried to put Jake on the table, Harry's mother said he must stay on the floor. When he tried to put him in the bath, his mother said he might catch cold. And when he tried to take him to bed, his mother said, 'No, Jake must sleep in his basket, in the kitchen.'

His mother explained that *real* puppies can't do all the things a pretend puppy does. 'But,' she said, 'there are plenty of things they can *both* do, like play with a ball, go for walks, and romp in the park.'

Harry explained this to Jake and Joe, and they both seemed quite happy about it. Harry is happy too, for now he has two pets, and there is always one of them with him.

# Chocolate biscuits!

Anne liked going shopping with her mother in the supermarket. She helped to push the trolley, and to get things down off the shelves.

They bought eggs, ham, sausages, cheese, washing-powder, fish-fingers, dog-biscuits, flour, apples, tins of peas, tins of beans, tomato sauce, and bread and butter. Then they came to the shelf that held Anne's favourite food: chocolate biscuits! Her mother always played a game with Anne, pretending to decide *not* to buy biscuits after all, and putting the packet back on the shelf.

Then Anne always said, 'Please, Mum, please! Just this once!'

And her mother said, 'Well, all right . . . Just this once!' Then she smiled and put the packet into the trolley.

One day, when they got home and went into the kitchen, their dog, Happy, jumped up and down as he always did, wagging his tail.

'You certainly live up to your name, Happy,' said Anne's mother, 'but I can't put these things away if you're jumping about all over the place. Anne, will you take Happy out and have a game with him?'

Anne loved playing with Happy, so they went out, and she threw a stick for him, again and again, and he chased after it, barking, and brought it back and put it down at her feet. After twenty minutes, Happy was so tired that he lay down on the ground, panting. Anne went back indoors.

There was no-one in the kitchen. She could hear her mother in the other room, laying the table. Then she saw that the door of one of the cupboards was open. It was the cupboard where her mother kept the biscuits.

'If I just take *one* chocolate biscuit, no-one will notice,' thought Anne. By standing on tip-toe and stretching her hands up above her head, she could just reach the right shelf. She felt for the packet, took out a biscuit, and quickly popped it in her mouth.

But when she bit on it, she let out a loud yell. It was so hard, she thought she had nearly broken a tooth. It was dry too, and tasted horrible. She put her hand to her mouth, and spat it out, just as her mother came into the kitchen, saying, 'Whatever's the matter?'

She looked at the bits of biscuit in Anne's hand, and at her screwed-up face, and started to laugh.

'Well, that just serves you right, Anne,' said her mother, 'for trying to take a biscuit without asking. Do you know what you took by mistake? One of Happy's dog-biscuits!'

# The baby hedgehog

Julie picked up the packet of sandwiches her mother had made and put them in her basket. Then she carefully stood the flask of hot chocolate beside them. Julie and her brother Benjamin were going fishing. They kissed their mother good-bye, then Benjamin picked up his fishing rod and they both set off down the lane that led to the river.

To get to the river they had to cross the main road. They looked both ways and when it was clear they hurried across. When they got to the other side Julie stopped. 'Oh look,' she said, 'it's a dead hedgehog. The poor little thing must have been run over.' She turned away sadly.

'Wait Julie, look,' called Benjamin, 'there's something else there.' Sure enough a little further down the road there was something that looked like a tennis ball covered with spikes.

'It's a baby hedgehog,' said Julie, stooping down to pick it up.

'Mind its prickles,' said Benjamin. 'Here, use one of my gloves.'

Julie took the glove and carefully picked up the little creature, but it was so young that its spines were not yet very sharp. 'We must take it home and look after it,' she said. They made their way straight home. Their mother was

quite surprised to see them back so soon.

'Hello again,' she said.

'We've found a baby hedgehog,' burst in Julie, holding out her hand.

'I thought you'd gone out to catch fish, not hedgehogs,' laughed her mother.

'Can we look after it until it's old enough to look after itself?' asked Julie.

'Of course,' said her mother. 'You'd better have this cardboard box, it'll make a nice house for him.'

They put some old leaves and twigs in the bottom of the box to make it nice and cosy and then carefully put the little hedgehog inside.

Their mother told them that in time the little hedgehog would leave them and go back to make its home in the woods.

'I know,' said Julie sadly, 'but I do hope it will remember to look both ways before it crosses the road.'

# Mother Christmas

One morning in December, when the snow was falling fast, Mother Christmas said to Father Christmas, 'You must brush your red suit and polish your boots, for soon it will be time for you to go on your Christmas journey'.

'Yes,' said Father Christmas, 'very soon now I must leave for the Earth again with a sleigh packed full of Christmas presents.'

So Father Christmas began to get his Christmas clothes all ready. He polished his tall black boots until he could see his face in them and brushed his bright red suit. Then Mother Christmas helped him to pack all the parcels.

Father Christmas went to bed early that night because he was very tired and he had a lot to do the next day. Mother Christmas sat up late sewing and sewing a great big cushion. She chuckled to herself as she filled the cushion with more and more soft, downy feathers. By the time she had finished it was nearly morning. She wrote something on a large label and tied it on to a silver tassel that hung from a corner of the cushion.

'This will be a surprise for Father Christmas,' she chuckled to herself, 'and I will put it in the sleigh just where he sits. I hope he looks at the label and reads, 'Not To Be Opened Until Christmas Day'. Then by the time he opens it he will be on his way back to me again.'

On Christmas Eve Father Christmas climbed into the sleigh and sat down on the soft silky parcel. 'Good gracious, whatever's this?' he said, and he got up and picked up the parcel. 'Not To Be Opened Until Christmas Day', he read. 'Then of course I mustn't open it. I must do as it says on the label,' he said.

That Christmas Eve Father Christmas was so busy delivering the presents that he almost forgot about his very own present. It wasn't until early on Christmas morning when he had finished his work that he remembered it. He opened it quickly and when all the wrapping had been laid aside Father Christmas lifted the label that hung from the silver tassel and read, 'With Love From Mother Christmas'.

He smiled and sat down on the soft cushion and whispered, so softly that even the reindeer could not hear, 'Dear Mother Christmas, how very kind of her to remember me, when she has all the children in the world to think about.'

# New friends

Debbie and her family were moving. 'The removal van is here,' her mummy called up the stairs.

Ebony was snoozing on Debbie's bed. Debbie gently picked up the black cat and popped her in the wicker basket.

At the new house, Debbie put down a saucer of milk, but Ebony rushed upstairs, and crept under Debbie's bed.

Debbie went into the garden and stared at the tall weeds. 'I can't play *here*!' she thought.

A little girl ran into the neat garden next door. 'I'm Tina. Would you like to play with me?' she asked. Eagerly, Debbie ran into Tina's garden.

Later, her mummy called, 'Dinner's ready, Debbie.'

'I must give Ebony her dinner first,' she said, and ran upstairs to fetch her cat. But when Debbie looked under her bed, Ebony wasn't there. Debbie ran downstairs.

'Perhaps she's in the garden. The kitchen door has been open all morning,' said Mummy.

In the garden, Debbie called and called. But Ebony didn't come.

As Debbie sat down to dinner, she saw a white cat come into her garden. 'I wish you were Ebony,' she sighed.

Then she stared. Something moved behind the white cat. It was black.

'It's Ebony! She's made a new friend too!' smiled Debbie happily.

# A lost lamb

A lamb went out all by himself one day. His mother was always telling him not to wander away but the lamb never took any notice.

He came to a wood. Oh, it was a lovely wood – there were beautiful tall trees, and soft green moss, and flowers.

The lamb thought, 'I would like to live here for ever and ever and ever.' He lay down on the moss and was soon fast asleep.

In the big green field his mother suddenly discovered that he was missing.

'He has run off again,' she thought. She ran up to Sam and Seth the sheep-dogs and told them about her missing lamb. Sam barked that he would go and search for him.

When the lamb woke up from his sleep it was getting dark. He did not know where he was, and suddenly he felt very scared. It is not much fun to be lost in a dark wood with the black night coming on.

Then he heard Sam's bark. 'Ba-Baaaaaaaaa!' called the little lost lamb, meaning, 'Sam! Sam! Here I am!'

Sam ran to where the lamb lay, a little patch of white in the deep shadows.

Grumbling at the lamb for straying so far from the fold, Sam took him all the way back to where his mother was waiting for him.

# Gary's adventure

'De-dah, de-dah,' shouted Gary as he raced around the garden in his police pedal car. Gary was very proud of his car because he wanted to be a policeman and drive a real police car when he grew up.

Later that day Gary went with his mummy into town. She was going shopping at the sales. Gary always held Mummy's hand very tightly, but the first shop they went into was so crowded that somehow Gary's hand slipped from Mummy's and he lost sight of her. Gary was pushed by the crowds back through the shop out on to the pavement. He couldn't get back into the shop and didn't know where he was. He was very frightened.

He walked for what seemed a long, long time then, luckily, he saw a policeman. Gary told the policeman who he was and what had happened.

Within two minutes a huge white police car pulled up beside the pavement. It had a large red stripe along each side and a big blue light on the roof.

'Jump in, Gary,' said the two policemen in the car. 'Your mummy is at the police station waiting for you.'

Gary climbed excitedly into the back seat of the police car. 'Please can you put on the siren and the flashing blue light?' he asked.

The driver laughed, 'No, we can't do that young man, they are only for emergencies.'

Suddenly, the radio crackled and a voice said, 'Q.36, will you go to the motorway where a petrol tanker has crashed.'

'That's us they're calling,' said the driver. 'We'll have to rush.'

'Oh, does that mean I can come?' asked Gary, his eyes glistening with excitement, 'Is this an emergency?'

'It is an emergency Gary, but I'm afraid you can't come. It will be very dangerous on the motorway. We shall have to really hurry to take you back to the police station first,' the driver explained.

Immediately the car began to go faster and faster, 'De-dah, de-dah, de-dah,' went the siren. Gary couldn't speak he was so excited. They raced straight down the middle of the High Street and all the other cars and lorries pulled out of their way.

It took them only two minutes to get to the police station but it was the most exciting two minutes of Gary's life.

'Thank you,' Gary shouted as he jumped out and ran to his mother. Gary felt very proud as he watched the police car race off down the hill. What an adventure he had to tell.

# Hippos and rhinos

There was a great splashing sound as a family of hippos played in the river.

'Come on in, the water's lovely,' they shouted to a lonely little figure who was standing at the water's edge. It was Tiny. He was the only one who didn't like swimming.

'No thanks, it's a bit too deep for me,' he said. But just in case they made fun of him he waded very carefully into the shallowest part, so that the water only came to his ankles.

'Fancy not liking the water,' laughed one of the larger hippos. 'I love it.'

While the big hippo was diving up and down Tiny crept away to find a tasty bush to nibble. This was much nicer, he thought to himself. It was awful when the other hippos pushed him into the water. It would go in his ears and eyes and once he was nearly eaten by a crocodile!

'Hello! What are you up to?' said a voice. Tiny looked round and saw a giraffe.

'Oh, just having my elevenses,' he said. As he spoke his nose began to feel itchy. Tiny rubbed it against a tree which made it feel better.

During the next few weeks he began to get a bump where the itchy part had been. All the other hippos made fun of it.

By the time the rainy season had come again Tiny's bump had grown into a lovely point. When he looked at his reflection in the water he could see another bump coming.

He was rather worried about this for none of the other hippos had pointy bits on their noses. So he decided to hide away from them. As he trotted along he saw some other hippos but they were odd just like he was. The smallest one looked friendly.

'Are you going swimming?' asked Tiny.

'No fear,' said the smallest animal. 'I only like water for drinking.'

'Most hippos love swimming,' said Tiny.

'I know, but I'm not a hippo. I'm like you, a rhinoceros.'

So that was it. At last Tiny knew why he hated going into the river. Now he could explain everything to the hippos.

'We are very sorry to have been so unkind to you,' the hippos told him. 'Please forgive us.'

Tiny did forgive them and then he proudly went off to join the other rhinos.

# William's book

William had been at school for two terms and liked it very much. He could write quite neatly, and was just beginning to read for himself.

One day William had an idea; he decided he would practice his writing by copying from one of his books. When he told his mum she had an even better idea. 'Why don't you write a book of your own?' she said.

At first William was not sure that he could do it. 'I couldn't think of enough things to fill a book,' he said, but his mum promised she would help him a bit to start with, so he decided to try.

His mum suggested that he made his book like a diary and wrote one page each day. 'You won't get tired of it then,' she said. As well as a book Mum bought him a sharp pencil with a rubber on the end and a box of shiny crayons. William just couldn't wait to begin.

He spent the evening designing the first page. He wrote

'My Diary' in large letters and then drew a bright pattern all round.

He hurried home from school the next day, and wrote 'Tuesday' at the top of a clean page, then he drew a picture of the puppet he'd made that afternoon, with a list of instructions underneath. Mum wrote the difficult words on a piece of paper for him to copy.

On the 'Wednesday' page he wrote about helping Mum with the baking and he added the special recipe for the flapjacks they'd made.

William's book was growing and growing. Nearly every day he could find something interesting to write about or draw: going fishing with Dad, the hedgehog they found in the garden and fed with bread and milk, the journey to Grandma's house by the sea. In no time at all he had reached the very last page.

'There, William,' said Mum. 'I knew you could write a book. What are you going to write on the last page?'
William grinned and wrote, 'End of Part One'.

# The silver sandals

A pair of silver sandals lay in Tracey's shoe cupboard, feeling very sorry for themselves. 'It really isn't fair!' they sighed. 'The other shoes, boots and slippers in the shoe cupboard are very useful to Tracey, but we don't seem to be any use to her at all.'

The silver sandals knew that on every wet day the red rubber boots were taken out of the cupboard. Tracey wore them when she played in the garden, and they kept her feet dry – even when she went splashing through puddles!

On school days, Tracey took her brown shoes out of the cupboard. They had straps and smart buckles, and they were strong and comfortable.

A pair of canvas play-shoes also lived in the cupboard. They were worn at weekends.

Every morning and every evening, Tracey wore her furry slippers. They were the same colour as her pink dressing-gown, and they kept her feet warm and cosy.

'You are all useful, except us!' sighed the silver sandals, one night.

The rubber boots, the school shoes, the play-shoes and the slippers all thought that the silver sandals were beautiful.

'You are the prettiest of all of us!' they said.

'But we don't want to be just *pretty*,' sighed the silver sandals. 'We want to be useful to Tracey.'

The very next morning, the silver sandals had a surprise. Tracey took them out of the shoe cupboard and polished them until they shone even more brightly than usual.

'I'm going to wear you to a party this afternoon,' said Tracey.

The silver sandals were delighted. 'A party! A party! We're going to a party!' they whispered to one another.

The silver sandals were so pleased and excited to be worn to a party, and they thought it wonderful fun.

Then, on the evening after the party, Tracey told the silver sandals that she was going to wear them to a wedding the very next Saturday – a *wedding*!

'You see,' the red boots said to the silver sandals, that night, in the shoe cupboard, 'you may not go out quite as often as the rest of us, but when you do, you go to very special places!'

# The rainbow jumper

It had been raining all day, and somehow everybody seemed cross and miserable, just like the weather. Mum couldn't hang the washing out for a blow and that always upset her. Dad couldn't get out into the garden and the flower beds badly needed weeding. Even Digger the spaniel looked sadder than usual; no walk for him after tea.

As for Sara, even the rainbow that she was looking for refused to appear. Mum had told her that you had to have sunshine and rain before you could have a rainbow, but Sara kept looking, and hoping.

She tried to do a puzzle but some of it was missing so there was a big hole in the middle; she pushed the pieces back into the box and shoved it to the back of her toy cupboard. And still no rainbow.

She took out her drawing books and started to colour a picture, but Sara wasn't very good at putting the tops back on her felt-tip pens and they'd all dried out. She put her colouring things back in her desk and looked out of her window again; still no rainbow.

For a while she played with her dolls, but she was all fingers and thumbs and kept getting their arms stuck in their sleeves and their hair tangled in their buttons. She was getting quite cross with herself and when she looked out of the window she began to think that Mum was right; there wasn't going to be a rainbow to cheer up this dreary wet day.

But Sara was wrong. In the middle of the afternoon there was a knock at the door and there stood Gran, smiling and wet and half hidden by a huge green umbrella. Gran had brought a present for Sara, something she'd been making, a surprise!

What a lovely surprise it was, for inside the bag that Gran had given her was the prettiest jumper Sara had ever seen. Gran had used up all her odd scraps of wool and had knitted the jumper in stripes, stripes that were all the colours of the rainbow!

'Well,' laughed Mum, 'you needn't keep looking out of the window now, Sara. You've got a rainbow of your very own'. And, whenever the weather was wet and gloomy, Sara would wear her rainbow jumper and brighten up the day.

# Rupert rat

There were six white rats living in a zoo. The keeper knew them all by their names, which were Rupert, Charlie, Daisy, Martha, Paula and John. Their cage was large with plenty of corners to hide in and they were given two good meals a day. So they were well looked after. But they did sometimes wish they could run into the wide world and see where the people who stared in at them lived.

One day the keeper left the door of the cage open by mistake. Daisy quickly spotted it and ran out, followed by the others. They found themselves in the passageway that ran behind their cage. Rupert sat down by a big door near a little dark hole in the floor. Suddenly the door opened, the keeper came in and shut it behind him quickly. It was now or never for escape! Rupert darted down the hole. Just in time. All the other rats were caught.

Rupert began to get tired and hungry. The tunnel seemed so large and seemed to go on for ever. Every so often his tunnel turned and was joined by others. So he was completely lost. He saw other rats. They were all brown or black and looked fierce, with eyes that gleamed in the dark.

Rupert tried to catch some pieces of cabbage that were

floating past, but a big brown rat got them first and pushed Rupert into the water. It was cold. But the sides were covered with green slime and too slippery to climb out. So Rupert floated down with the current.

Just as he had begun to give up hope the water from the drain swept into a big river and out into the daylight. Rupert saw an old black boot floating along and he climbed on the toe, getting a little warmer and drier in the sunshine.

The boot reached the side of the river. Rupert jumped off and sat in the grass. A lot of people were sitting there and talking, which frightened Rupert a bit, but there were crumbs on the ground so he crept forward and ate some.

Suddenly he was in complete darkness again! Someone had put their hat on top of him. Then a little boy's hand caught Rupert firmly. He was a prisoner again.

But the little boy took Rupert home and he was given a big cage with some hamsters for company and *three* good meals a day. So he did not try to escape again!

# The seaside camel

At first Hamid the camel liked his life by the sea in Tunisia. It was spring and there weren't many visitors, because it wasn't very hot yet. When summer came Hamid began to wish he was a desert camel, not a seaside camel. There were hundreds of visitors, all wanting to clamber on to his back and have their photographs taken.

All the seaside camels liked to go for treks along the river valleys; it was much cooler and far more interesting than walking along the beach. Every morning they lined up hoping to be picked to take the tourists on the trek. Hamid had been several times and he never tired of the journey, although it took the whole morning.

One morning a little girl called Helen came running up to Hamid as he waited in the line. She liked his bright striped blanket beneath the saddle. 'Oh please let me ride this camel,' she cried to her daddy.

Hamid knew the way. He set off slowly and gently along the dried-up river bed. Helen had squealed when they started off. She didn't know that camels tipped forward and got up on to their back legs first, then tipped backwards as they straightened their front legs. Hamid realised he would have to be careful not to frighten Helen.

The camel train rounded a bend in the river. Only one more bend and they would reach the citrus farm and Hamid could have a rest beneath a shady tree.

At the citrus farm the tourists drank orange and lemon drinks made from fresh oranges and lemons.

The sun began to get hotter and Hamid snorted to remind his master it was time to start for home. He was thirsty and when he came to a water trough Hamid stopped and started to drink. His master was very cross. All the other camels were getting further and further ahead.

Hamid decided he had better catch up with the others and started to trot. He could feel Helen hanging on to his neck. He was afraid his master would not let him carry any more children if he scared Helen, and he was very pleased to hear her say, just as he was taken into his stable for a well earned rest, 'I did enjoy my camel ride.'

# The dream

Lisa was having a lovely time. She was riding very fast in a great big car down a beautiful glittery avenue. The trees on either side were like willow trees, only the leaves were silver, and from each branch hung a big, sticky bun. As the car sped along, Lisa reached out her hand and, with no trouble at all, picked one of the buns from a tree.

A gruff voice beside her said, 'A pretty nice place this, isn't it?'

She looked down and there beside her on the seat sat her cat Blinkers, smiling up at her and cleaning his whiskers. He had just eaten a big, sticky bun too.

'Oh look,' said Blinkers, and pointed his paw ahead. There in front of them lay a shimmering lake surrounded by the silver trees.

'Goodness,' said Lisa, as the car wove between the trees, 'we're going to go straight in.'

'Wake up darling. It's time to get dressed for school,' said a voice from a long way off. Lisa stretched and yawned.

'Oh Mummy, I've had such a lovely, exciting dream,' she said. She felt a weight on her leg. It was Blinkers. He stretched and yawned too, and for a moment she almost thought he winked at her.

# The stone lion

Benjamin, a well behaved lion, was asked to guard the entrance to a palace because one of the stone lions who usually sat outside the doors was having his nose mended.

This was a great honour for Benjamin and he willingly took up his position, sitting on his hind legs and staring out at the world.

He'd been given a list of 'Don'ts' . . .

Don't growl at visitors.

Don't scratch.

Don't lie down.

Don't blink.

In other words, behave at all times like a stone lion.

Benjamin performed his duty day in day out until he really did begin to feel like a stone lion.

One day a van arrived to return the real stone lion, which now had a new nose. Benjamin could hardly move because he'd been sitting still for so long.

It took three weeks before he felt really lively again. And ever afterwards he was known in the jungle for his ability to sit very, very still!

Why don't you try being a stone lion?

# The Big Top

Early one sunny morning, a little boy named David was woken up by a loud noise on the road outside. 'I wonder what that is?' he thought to himself. And he looked through the window to see.

There, rumbling and grumbling along, were five long lorries. They were driving towards the big field at the bottom of David's road. The little boy ran downstairs to the kitchen where his mother was making breakfast. 'Did you see those lorries, Mummy?' he asked.

'Yes,' she said, 'didn't they make a lot of noise! I wonder why they're going into the big field?'

'Can I go with Steven to find out?' David asked.

'After breakfast,' his mother told him.

So, after breakfast, David ran along the road to call for his best friend, Steven, and together they went on until they came to the big field. What a bustle there was! The lorries were being unloaded, and men were running here and there with boxes and bundles of every shape and size. At the

entrance to the field there was a big sign. 'Baggolini's Circus,' it said.

'A circus!' cried David.

'A *real* circus!' cried Steven.

Just then, the two boys heard someone behind them. It was the circus Ringmaster! He wore a black top hat, as shiny as his boots, a red coat and black trousers, and he had a long whip in his hand.

'Hello, you two,' he said to David and Steven. 'Would you like to help? We're going to put up the Big Top.'

'What's the Big Top?' asked David.

'It's the big round circus tent,' said the Ringmaster. 'Come along, I'll show you what to do.'

So David and Steven followed the Ringmaster into the big field and they helped the men to carry the ropes and boxes. Then they helped to put up the Big Top. It grew higher and higher into the sky as the men pulled on the ropes.

At last the work was finished and the Big Top stood ready in the field. The Ringmaster was very pleased with David and Steven. 'Thank you for helping us,' he said. 'Here you are – free tickets for the circus show tonight. I'm sure you'll enjoy yourselves.'

And he was right – they did.

# A black cat

Snowflake was a beautiful, silky-haired white cat. She was rather fat and had large green eyes and very long hair, and she lived with a little girl called Katy and her parents in a little cottage in the country.

One evening Katy was worried because Snowflake didn't come when she called her.

'Don't worry Katy,' said Daddy. 'I'll look for Snowflake after you've gone to bed. She can't have gone far because it's chilly outside.'

Daddy went outside later with his torch and called, 'Snowflake! Snowflake!'

It was very cold outside and the wind was howling. He hugged his coat round him and went back inside.

'No sign of her,' he said to Katy's mother.

'Oh dear,' Mummy replied. 'I hope she hasn't got lost.'

Katy was very sad the next morning when she discovered Snowflake hadn't returned, and even sadder the following day when there was still no sign of her cat.

The next day the coalman called. He was big and tall with

a very dirty face because when he tipped the coal into the coal sheds, great clouds of it rose up and covered him in dust.

'Good morning,' he said to Katy's mother. 'Where do I put the coal?'

'Thank goodness you've come,' she replied. 'We ran out of coal a week ago, and it's got so cold. Katy – you show the coalman where to put the coal.'

Katy led the coalman round to the back of the house to the coal shed. The coalman opened the little door and peered in. At that moment there was a loud 'miaow!'

'Bless my soul!' said the coalman.

'Snowflake!' said Katy.

Out ran a little black cat.

'Oh,' Katy said in disappointment. 'It's not Snowflake at all. It's a black cat. Still, it looks very hungry so I'll take it in and give it some milk.'

The cat purred a great deal when Katy picked her up and took her indoors.

'I've found a black cat in the coal shed, Mummy,' said Katy.

Mummy took a look at the purring cat and laughed. 'Silly,' she said. 'It's Snowflake!' She picked up an old cloth and rubbed it on the cat's back. 'Look!' she cried. 'She's all covered in soot – that's why she looks black. She must have got shut in the coal shed and as we ran out of coal we haven't been in there for a few days.'

# Doreen's quilt

Doreen was a lonely little girl. Her mother and father were busy, famous people, and she could watch them on television most afternoons. She lived in a big, grand house, set in its own gardens.

But there were rooms in the house which she wasn't allowed to use. In these rooms the carpets were white or grey. The walls were pale green or pale blue or pale pink.

The front part of the garden was also forbidden, with its tidy green lawns, and beds of purple and white and yellow flowers.

Doreen ate her meals in the kitchen with Mary the cook, who felt sorry for the lonely little girl. Doreen was allowed to play in the back garden where there was a swing, and a sand pit. But only Mary the cook, or Nellie the maid, ever had time to talk to her and tell her stories.

When Doreen's mother and father were away in another city, and they were often away, Mary had a special way of amusing the little girl.

She would clear the big kitchen table, and on this she would place a linen sheet that was not needed. Then as Nellie the maid cut out scraps of material, Mary and

Doreen would arrange them in patterns on the sheet.

In each corner they had made a cat of black velvet, with white satin whiskers, and blue eyes. In the centre was a huge sun-flower made from two of Doreen's worn-out summer frocks, one golden silk, the other one, green cotton.

When her mother and father were having a party, Doreen would sit in her pretty bedroom, and happily draw with her colouring pencils in her drawing-book.

Nellie would run upstairs with her supper on a tray, and would tell her to be a good little girl, and stay in her room. An hour later Nellie would run upstairs again, to help Doreen undress, and get ready for bed.

When she was by herself, Doreen would think out all the things she wanted on her quilt. A brown dog made from last winter's furry coat. Two pink rabbits made from her too-short dressing-gown.

To please her, Nellie promised to give her her blue satin dance frock, after she had worn it four more times. Doreen spent days thinking out what could be made from a large blue satin frock.

Would it be a sea all round the quilt, with boats on the sea? Or would it be the sky, with white clouds, and sea-gulls? Doreen could not make up her mind. Mary and Nellie would have to decide. What do you think?

# Cuthbert kitten

Cuthbert Kitten was one of those animals who just couldn't keep out of mischief! He walked through his saucer of milk every day and left sticky little footprints all over the kitchen floor. He hid under the settee and jumped out at anyone who passed.

'Oh, Cuthbert Kitten,' Annie cried when he laddered her tights for the second time in a day. 'Just wait till I catch you.'

Cuthbert didn't wait. He jumped up on to a chair then on to the windowsill and whoops! Over went the vase of flowers.

'Oh, Cuthbert Kitten,' Annie wailed. '*Now* look what you've done!'

While Annie was mopping up the spilt water Cuthbert ran into the hall and looked up the stairs. What an adventure it would be to climb all the way up, he thought.

When he got to the top of the stairs he looked around. All the doors were closed except one, which was open just a teeny, tiny bit. It was the boxroom where all the junk was stored. Cuthbert Kitten had a lovely time nosing into everything. Then he heard Annie coming. He hid behind a

big box and kept very still. Then he heard Annie go out of the room again. But, oh dear, she had closed the door!

It was a long, long time before Annie came back upstairs. In fact, it wasn't until she was on her way to bed. Then she heard him mewing and opened the boxroom door.

'Why, bless my soul, whatever are you doing here, Cuthbert Kitten?' she asked in surprise. 'We thought you were lost. How did you get here, anyway? Cats don't belong upstairs.'

She carried him downstairs and gave him a saucer of milk. After he had lapped it all up she put him in his nice warm basket. Cuthbert *was* glad Annie had found him.

'Now don't you get up to any more tricks, Cuthbert Kitten,' Annie said to him. And he didn't – at least, not *that* night!

# Horace helps out

The sun was just beginning to peep over the tops of the houses. Horace Hedgehog had been out all night, sniffing around the sheds in a big allotment looking for food.

He crawled through a gap in a thick hedge and saw he was in a large garden. He saw an old shed in one corner and went to look. He found a nice 'hedgehog sized' hole and climbed into the shed. 'My, it's nice and warm and dark in here,' he said, as he settled down behind some boxes for his sleep.

Just as he was dozing off, Horace heard a voice say, 'Shoo! Go away you naughty mice.'

'I'm not a mouse,' replied Horace, although he didn't know who he was talking to, 'I'm a tired hedgehog.'

At that moment a tortoise came around to the back of the boxes. 'Oh, I do beg your pardon,' said the tortoise wearily, 'I'm tired as well. Those naughty mice have been jumping and dancing on my shell all night long. They do it every night. I haven't had a wink of sleep.'

Horace felt sorry for the tortoise. 'I think I can help you,' he said.

The next night, Horace Hedgehog settled down exactly where the tortoise usually slept. When all the mice jumped on his back, they were so startled at finding sharp prickles under their feet instead of a smooth shell they ran away and never came back!

# The clean pig

Dapper was a very fussy pig. Although he lived in a sty with all the other pigs he didn't care for their dirty habits – snorting, pushing and rooting around in the muck.

'I was pink as a piglet!' he shouted over the sty wall, 'and now look at me – I'm a sort of nasty patchy colour.'

He shouted again, 'Why must I live in this awful smelly place? I want to be clean. I want a bath.'

'Feel free to use my trough,' Thomas the horse suggested.

'How kind,' smiled Dapper, 'I'll have a bath straightaway.'

Dapper had a lovely bath in the horse trough and came out all pink. He rolled in the grass to dry off. Then back he trotted to the sty.

'Phew, Dapper's so dirty he's turning green and mouldy,' said the pigs.

'*I've* just had a bath!' Dapper insisted.

'Well, you are all green!' said the other pigs.

When Dapper had rolled in the grass, it had stained him green all over.

How the other pigs laughed. Now Dapper doesn't go on about being clean so much any more!

# The lost ball

There once lived a little girl, Kay, who had a brown dog called Bertie. One morning, Kay said, 'Happy Birthday, Bertie. Did you know it's your special day today?'

'Woof!' said Bertie, and he wagged his tail.

'Look what I've got for you,' said Kay. And she opened a paper bag and brought out – a big yellow ball.

'Woof-woof!' said Bertie, and his tail wagged faster than ever.

'After breakfast, we'll go for a walk in the field and play with your new ball,' Kay said. And so they did.

For a while they played throw-and-catch. Then Kay decided it was time for hide-and-seek. So while Bertie lay down on the grass, the little girl hid the ball behind a tree nearby. 'Find it, Bertie!' she said. And he did.

Then it was Bertie's turn. He carried the ball in his mouth looking for a good place to hide it. Among the roots of the tree was a dark hole. That would make a good hiding place! Bertie dropped the yellow ball into the hole. But – oh dear! – it rolled right out of sight. 'Woof!' barked Bertie loudly. 'Woof-woof!'

Kay came running up. 'Oh Bertie, where's your ball?' she asked. Then she saw the hole. 'Naughty dog, have you lost it down that rabbit hole? Now we won't be able to get it out again.'

And she was right – they couldn't. They had to leave the yellow ball behind. And that evening when her father came home, the little girl told him what had happened.

'Don't worry, Kay,' he said. 'I know how we can get the ball back.' After tea, Kay's father looked in a cupboard and found an old walking stick.

When they reached the spot where the rabbit hole was, Kay's father pushed the curly handle of the walking stick into the hole.

'What are you doing?' cried Kay.

'Wait and see,' said her father. When the walking stick was a little way down the hole he began to pull it out again, very carefully. And there, hooked inside the curly handle, was Bertie's yellow ball!

'Woof-woof!' barked Bertie happily, wagging his rail.

'Fetch it!' cried Kay, and she threw the ball high into the air. Bertie chased after it, and when he caught it he carried it in his mouth all the way home and put it in his basket.

After that he took the greatest care not to lose his yellow ball again.

# Little Bear

Little Bear was wide awake. His mother, brother and sister were all very sleepy for winter was drawing near and bears hibernate in the winter. The days were growing colder and the nights darker and longer.

'Come to bed, Little Bear,' said his mother.

But Little Bear took no notice. He went on playing. He jumped, turned somersaults and kept his family wide awake when they wished to sleep.

Then he caught sight of the honey-jar his mother had found in the forest. Mother Bear had brought the jar full of honey home with her, and had told her children, 'We will save this for when we wake up hungry in the spring.'

Little Bear did not want to wait till then, and seeing that his family were nearly asleep, he pulled down the honey-pot, and stuck his nose inside.

Then he found that he could not get it out.

'Owwww-yow-yow,' he yelled. 'Mama, Mama, come and help me.'

Mother Bear, was wide awake by now because of the noise Little Bear was making. She got up and managed to get his nose free of the honey-pot.

'Now go to sleep, you bothersome bear,' she said.

'I'm not tired,' whined Little Bear.

'Yes you are, but you don't know it. Shut your eyes. Tight. Tighter.'

Little Bear screwed up his eyes obediently. He could hear the gentle snores of his brother and sister – they were fast asleep by now.

'Oh well,' thought Little Bear, 'I suppose I am a little bit tired,' and with this last thought, Little Bear fell fast asleep.

# Riding lessons

More than anything Robert wanted to have riding lessons. When he asked Mummy she said that riding lessons were rather expensive, but she would see what could be done.

Robert made a special plan of his own. He decided to try and earn some money.

First he helped the neighbours by looking after their rabbits while they were on holiday. Then he took Aunty Sally's dog for walks.

All this helpfulness brought him lots of extra pocket money. Soon he had enough money to pay for the first riding lesson.

He took his money to Mummy and she was very proud of him. Daddy said he had been such a good boy that he would give him the money for more lessons, if he promised to carry on helping.

It wasn't long before Robert was one of the best riders in the riding school.

# The teapot toad

I suppose you know how fond most toads are of living under damp stones. But the toad in this story didn't like damp stones. He found himself an old teapot, set on the top of a hill, to live in instead. To him it was like having a huge mansion.

Other toads whispered that Bartholomew only needed a horse and carriage and he'd think himself the squire of the county!

'He thinks he is too good for us,' they said. 'Let's persuade him to move down here under the rocks with us!'

A party of them went up to see Bartholomew, who agreed

on the condition that he brought his 'mansion' with him.

It took twelve toads six hours to move the mansion while Bartholomew shouted instructions to them. Suddenly they all lost their tempers with him and just let the teapot roll over and over until it broke into a thousand pieces.

'That was my *home*,' Bartholomew wailed.

'Too bad,' they said, 'you can live down here in the valley with us, where you really belong.'

'Not likely,' answered Bartholomew. 'Because, silly, jealous toads, the laugh is on you. That teapot was part of an old teaset. I've got a milk jug, four cups, and a sugar bowl all nicely stacked away in different parts of the country – in fact I've got another six country mansions. Goodbye!' And off he hopped.

# Snowy

Snowy was Angela's birthday present. He was a little white fluffy teddy bear. Angela loved him very much. He was so white that she had called him Snowy, and he went everywhere with her. He went with her to school and out with her to play and when Angela had her bath Snowy had a bath, too, so he was always very white and clean.

One cold winter's day Angela came running into the kitchen. 'Oh Mummy,' she sobbed, 'I've lost Snowy. I'll never find him. We were playing and . . . and I must have dropped him in the snow. He's so white I'll never be able to find him!'

'Now calm down Angie,' said her mother kindly. 'If you and I go out looking together I'm sure we'll find him. You just dry your eyes while I fetch my hat and coat and my warm boots.'

Angela sobbed quietly as they walked together over to the meadow where the children had been playing. The snow was thick on the ground like a big white blanket. As they crossed the tiny bridge over the river Angela's mother saw a swan floating gracefully over to the river's edge. 'Look at that beautiful swan, Angie. What colour is it?' asked her mother.

'It's white, Mummy, you know it's white just like Snowy,' Angela said and she started to cry again.

Her mother pretended not to notice her tears. 'Look Angie, look at the swan now, it's climbing up the river bank on to the snow. Is it still white?'

'Of course it is,' sobbed Angela without even looking. But when she did look, what a surprise she had. Swans were white, Angela knew that, but this swan certainly didn't look white now. It looked more a yellowy colour. 'It doesn't look very white against the snow, does it Mummy?' she said.

'No Angie, it doesn't. Nothing is quite as white as snow. I think we'll find your Snowy quite easily. Let's start looking.'

Angela rushed off to where the children had been making their snowman. Her mother followed her looking carefully all around.

'Look Angie, over there, something lying in the snow,' called her mother. 'It could be . . .' Angela ran off before her mother could finish.

'It's him, Mummy, it's him,' cried Angela. 'Oh Mummy, we've found him after all!'

# Soap and dumplings!

One cold winter's day Mummy made a stew for tea.

'Stew and dumplings!' she told John and Diana.

'Goody!' they cried. It was dark outside, and they were hungry.

Suddenly, all the lights went out.

'Oh dear!' said Mummy, 'A power cut! We will have to light candles.' She rummaged in the dark. 'I can only find one,' she said.

'It's time,' said Mummy, 'to do the dumplings, and I can hardly see what I'm doing.' She took the lid off the stew and put it on the draining board, while she peered in the gloom and dropped dumplings into the stew.

Then Daddy came home. 'What's this?' he said. 'Is the electricity off again?'

'Yes,' said Mummy, 'and we only have one candle.'

'I'll get more tomorrow,' said Daddy, taking his coat off.

'Tomorrow isn't *now*,' said Mummy.

Daddy grinned. 'Where's the soap?' he said, running the tap.

'It's there somewhere,' said Mummy, 'you will have to *feel* for it!'

Daddy tried, but could not find the piece of soap.

'Well, never mind for now,' said Mummy. 'These

dumplings will be ready in a minute, so just rinse your hands, instead.'

Suddenly, Mummy gave a great wail. 'Oh!' she cried, 'Oh *look*, – look at this stew!' They all came to look, and Daddy brought the candle near, to see better.

The stew looked very peculiar, it was frothing in a funny way. And then they spied a piece of pink soap, merrily bubbling amongst the dumplings. How they all laughed and laughed – except Mummy!

'Won't our insides smell *nice*!' said John, rolling on a chair.

'And be ever so *clean*!' giggled Diana.

Daddy wiped the tears from his face, and looked at the pan lid. 'See!' he said, 'You must have put the lid on top of the soap in the dark, and the soap stuck to it – then dropped into the stew!'

'Well,' said Mummy, 'you can all stop laughing your heads off. This means you have nothing to eat for your tea!'

But they opened some tins, and managed with tinned food instead. It wasn't as nice as stew and dumplings though!

# The sad donkey

Derry was a very sad old donkey. He was sad because he was lonely. Once, when he'd been young, he'd lived at the seaside and had taken children for rides along the sands all summer. Derry had liked that.

He'd liked living in the country, too, at first, when he had been the children's pet and they had played with him every day. But now they were nearly grown-up and weren't often at home and poor Derry spent most of his days alone in the paddock dreaming of the happy times he'd had when he was young.

One cold winter's day, he was standing in a corner of the paddock feeling very lonely and sad when suddenly he pricked up his ears. He could hear children's voices. His master and another man appeared at the gate of the paddock with a whole crowd of children.

His master said, 'That's Derry. He's used to children . . . gentle as a lamb!'

'Oh, isn't he lovely?' the boys and girls said.

The other man smiled and said to the children, 'Well, shall we give Derry a part in our Christmas play?'

'Yes, yes!' they all shouted excitedly and they followed the man through the gate into the paddock and crowded around Derry, patting and stroking him. He wondered what was happening.

After a while they led him round to the big old barn and began to act the play they were rehearsing for Christmas. A little girl they called Mary had to ride on his back and a nice boy they called Joseph had to lead Derry across one end of the barn.

There were more rehearsals during the next two weeks. Derry looked forward to them. All the children talked to him and stroked him and sometimes they brought him apples. He didn't feel lonely any more.

At last the day came when the children were to perform their Nativity play in the barn for their parents and brothers and sisters and friends.

Derry walked slowly into the barn with the little girl called Mary on his back. Everyone in the audience said, 'Aahhhhhh,' and a little girl shouted excitedly, 'Ooh, look – a *real* donkey!'

Derry felt very proud. While all the children sang 'Away in a Manger' he stood very still, looking into the crib where Mary had put a baby doll she called Jesus.

After that, the children often came to visit Derry in his field, and every year he took part in their Christmas play.

# The snow cake

Amanda was so excited the night before her birthday that she could hardly sleep. During the night it snowed and snowed very hard. What a surprise Amanda had when she woke up in the morning and saw all the snow!

She had a lovely time opening all her cards and presents. Then she decided to go and play outside in the garden in the crisp white snow.

She made a little snowman at the edge of the path. Then she had a good idea. She would pretend it was the snowman's birthday as well and make him a big white cake just like the one her mummy had made for her. So she made a great big snow-cake with patterns round the edge. Then she made a figure five on the top and stuck in five sticks for pretend candles.

When she had finished it was time to go inside and light the candles on her *real* birthday cake.

# The potato plant

Once there was a dusty brown potato. It was small and wrinkled and plain. Jonathan Jones planted it in his small garden patch.

One fine day a tiny green shoot began to poke its way up through the dark earth.

Jon's mother said, 'I wonder what this will be.'

A few weeks later, up came a beautiful spreading green plant.

Jon's mother said, 'Well, what do you think it will be, Jonathan?'

Jon said to his mother, 'We must just wait and see, mustn't we?'

A week or so later some pretty, pale, butterfly-mauve flowers appeared and, 'Well I never!' said Jon's mother. 'Do you know what this flower is called, Jon?'

Jon replied, 'Yes, but if I told you, it wouldn't be a surprise.'

The pretty mauve butterfly-flowers faded and dropped off the green foliage.

'Well,' said Mrs Jones, 'what do we do now?'

'Watch me,' said Jon and began to tug at the plant. Up and out of the ground it came, dropping little bits of earth.

Jon's mother stared in surprise for, at the bottom of the root, there hung ten, little, brown, new potatoes.

# Pink

Of all the colours, Sandra loved pink the best. She always wore a pink dress and a pretty pink ribbon in her hair.

Sandra liked the people next door because pink was their favourite colour too. In the spring, their garden was full of sweetly scented pink hyacinths. In the summer, their pink roses were lovely. Their pink chrysanthemums brightened the dull days of autumn. And in winter, when there were no real flowers, they put pink paper ones in vases on their windowsills.

Sandra called the people who lived next door Uncle Bob and Auntie May. Every evening, when Uncle Bob came into the garden, he looked over his fence and smiled. Then he gave her two sweeties. They were *always* pink, and tasted of spearmint. Sandra liked them very much.

One Saturday, in early summer, she went into the garden as usual, and waited for Uncle Bob. She waited until bedtime, but he didn't come.

Every evening for a whole week, Sandra waited for him, and every evening she grew sadder and sadder.

Sandra missed her two pink sweeties but, most of all, she missed Uncle Bob. Perhaps he and Auntie May had gone away for good, and she would never see them again.

It was on the Monday morning when at last she found out why they had gone away. As she ran downstairs a card fell through the letterbox. Sandra picked it up, and stared at the picture of a sandy beach.

'Mummy! Someone has sent us a picture postcard!' she cried, as she took it into the kitchen.

Her mummy smiled, and looked at the writing. 'It's from Uncle Bob. He and Auntie May are enjoying themselves in Devon. He sends you his love and looks forward to seeing you on Saturday.'

At last Saturday came. The little girl stood at the window and saw the car stop outside the house next door.

She pressed her nose against the glass as Uncle Bob and Auntie May got out of the car.

It was not long before Uncle Bob came to see her.

He held his hands behind his back. He smiled at the little girl, and his face was brown with the sun. 'Hello, Sandra. Look, we've brought you back a present.'

Sandra stared with delight. In Uncle Bob's hand was the biggest stick of pink rock she had ever seen!

# Mandy's zoo

One morning as Mandy was playing with her puppy Honey, she heard her daddy's car, and ran to the gate. He was a country vet. Sometimes, he brought home a new pet for her.

Mandy stared into the back of the car. There, asleep in a cardboard box, were three little black kittens. 'Are they for me?' Mandy asked.

Her daddy grinned. 'Yes, if your mummy will let you keep them,' he said.

Mandy went into the garden to feed the other animals. She gave Bobbin, the rabbit, some carrots. Horace the tortoise liked lettuce leaves.

Jackie the jackdaw hopped excitedly on his perch when he saw his seeds. His leg was better and soon he'd fly away.

In the afternoon, Mandy took Honey to the wood at the end of the garden.

Mandy threw a stick. Joyfully Honey ran to fetch it, then dropped it at the little girl's feet.

Again and again she threw the stick, and Honey brought

it back. Until Mandy threw it extra hard, and the stick landed in a bush.

Honey dived in and nosed around, but she couldn't find it. Then she barked excitedly.

'Have you found something?' Mandy asked, and ran to the bush. She gasped with surprise when she saw the little brown foxcub. 'Oh, you poor thing!' she said, and carried him home.

Her mummy stared at the tiny creature. 'He's lost his mummy. We'll care for him until he can look after himself,' she said.

As she put the foxcub on clean straw in an empty cage in the garden, she smiled. 'This gets more like a zoo every day. All we need is an elephant.'

Someone opened the gate at the bottom of the garden. They looked up in surprise.

Mandy's daddy held a rope. Something big and grey with a long trunk walked behind him. Mandy and her mummy gasped with surprise.

Daddy explained. 'The circus has left town,' he said. 'Sadie is too old to work now. So I'm looking after her until the people from the zoo come to collect her later today.'

'You must have heard me,' laughed Mandy's mummy. 'I said all we need is an elephant.'

Sadie must have seen the joke too, because she trumpeted loudly.

# The baby rabbits

'I'm sorry but I don't think I can come out today,' said Bobby Rabbit to his friend Mole. 'I have to look after my baby brothers and sisters while my mother is away.'

'Well, why can't we take them out with us?' said Mole. 'I'll help you to amuse them.'

'Well,' said Bobby doubtfully, 'they're very naughty, but perhaps some lively games will tire them out.'

So with the baby rabbits frisking round them, they set off towards the lake. After a while Mole looked round. 'Bobby,' he said. 'How many should there be?'

'Er . . . let me see, five I think. There's Sandy, Katie, Maggie, Georgie and Jeremy.'

'Well, there's only four here,' said Mole.

'Oh dear! Jeremy's gone. We must find him. Mother will be so worried.'

By now they had reached the lake, and Georgie suddenly cried, 'Look! There he is, floating along on that log. He's waving to us. Isn't he clever?'

'He's not clever at all,' said Bobby. 'He's floating towards the waterfall, and any minute he'll fall off. What shall we do?'

Just then, a small black head appeared above the water. 'Don't worry,' said Sammy Otter. 'I'll get him.' And in a flash he'd reached the log and pushed it to the shore.

'Thank you Sammy,' said Bobby. He turned round to call

the others. 'Oh dear!' he said. 'Katie isn't here now. This is too much. Where can she be?'

By now they'd reached a gardener's shed, and could hear scratching and squeaking coming from inside. 'That's her,' said Bobby. 'Katie, are you there? Come out at once.'

'I can't,' said Katie. 'I've eaten a lot of seeds, and now I'm too fat to get out.'

'Come on everyone, start digging,' Bobby cried. 'We must make a tunnel for her. Katie, you scrape on your side.'

They had nearly finished when they heard someone coming. It was Mr Potts the gardener! The rabbits hid behind the shed as Mr Potts opened the door and went in.

'Oh, so it's you whose been eating my seeds?' they heard him say. And then such a chasing and scuffling went on inside, until Mr Potts shouted, 'Got you,' and then with a cry of pain he yelled, 'Aah . . . it's bitten me!' He dropped Katie, who landed with a bump on the ground.

'Quick Katie, the tunnel's ready,' cried Bobby, and in a moment she was out, and they all bolted down the nearest rabbit hole.

Mother Rabbit was back when they got home. 'Oh, my dear little babies,' she said. 'Have you all been good? Of course, I know you have.'

'I don't suppose she would believe me if I told her what had happened, or she'd say it was my fault for not looking after them properly,' said Bobby. 'Well, they're all back safely. Come along Moley, let's go out by ourselves.'

# 'The Cherry House'

John and Jane had a new baby brother called Michael. Since Michael was born Mummy said that they were 'bursting at the seams'. Jane thought that sounded very funny and didn't really understand what Mummy meant.

'Well, you see,' said Mummy, 'we need a larger house. Granny can't come and stay with us now for we haven't enough bedrooms. I think we will have to move house.'

John and Jane were sad that their parents should want to move. They loved their present house. And they had many friends nearby, and didn't want to move away from them.

For a long time, on Saturdays, they went visiting other houses. Some of them Daddy and Mummy said were not suitable. One or two houses the children liked but their parents didn't. Altogether the children found it a boring occupation.

The winter passed and the spring came. The blossom on the trees was very beautiful – in particular the cherry blossom on the tree in the garden four doors down from John and Jane's house. This was where Mr and Mrs White and their son Paul lived. They had a lovely big house, and a big garden. Paul got married in the spring and that left just Mr and Mrs White living in 'The Cherry House', as John and Jane called it.

One evening when the children were in bed, the door bell rang. They didn't recognise the voices talking to their parents and the next morning there seemed to be something secret and mysterious happening. When they asked what the secret was, Daddy would only say, 'Wait and see.'

A few weeks later Daddy said that a new house had been found and that they would be moving in soon.

John said he was not moving and that he was going to hide

at the bottom of the garden for ever. Mummy laughed and said, 'You'll love our new home. After tea today we are going to see it.'

It was two very unhappy children who, after tea, were told to put their coats on.

'How far away is it?' asked John crossly.

'Not far,' said Mummy.

John and Jane slowly followed their parents down the road, dragging their feet. Suddenly Daddy stopped at 'The Cherry House'. At the front door Mr and Mrs White were waiting to let them in.

At last Jane and John understood all the mystery. 'The Cherry House' was too large now for Mr and Mrs White, but it was just right for Daddy, Mummy and the three children, and Granny when she came to stay. So John and Jane were quite happy to move after all.

# Martin at school

Miss Timmins's nursery class was the happiest in the whole school, or it was until Martin arrived.

Most children love school, but not Martin. He cried and screamed every day. 'I want to go home,' he shouted, until poor Miss Timmins didn't know what to do.

One morning Miss Timmins was giving out the milk when she came to Martin's place and saw that he had gone. She looked everywhere. At last she reached the kitchen, and there was Martin sitting on a table with a cake in his hand.

'Here I am,' he cried, waving the cake. 'You didn't tell me my Aunty Rose was here.'

Aunty Rose was the school cook, and she was very sorry when she heard how naughty Martin had been.

'You must go back to your teacher at once,' she said.

'No, I want to stay here,' he shouted. 'I want . . .'

'Martin, that's enough,' interrupted Aunty sternly.

'Now listen,' said Miss Timmins. 'If you promise to come back to the classroom quietly, then you may see your Aunty every playtime this week.'

So Martin promised, and began to enjoy coming to school.

After three days he said, 'I can't come tomorrow Aunty. I'm too busy helping teacher. I have to feed the goldfish every playtime now. Do you mind?'

'Of course not,' said Aunty Rose smiling. 'I understand.'

# Kidnap!

Gertrude Goat was feeling very happy as she trotted along by the side of her friend Gregory. Her two little kids were in the meadow playing together quite safely. At least that's what Gertrude thought they were doing.

It so happened that, unknown to Gertrude, two suspicious looking men were opening the gate that led into the meadow.

'There you are Sam, I reckon we can steal those kids easily,' said Sid.

The two kids were very frightened and ran away as fast as they could. But the men ran even faster and soon caught them. The little kids made a loud bleating calling for help.

Gertrude and Gregory were just finishing a tasty morsel when they heard the kids.

'Come on,' said Gregory. 'We haven't a moment to lose.'

Down to the meadow they ran and through the gate. Gregory had a most marvellous pair of horns. He gave Sid and Sam such a big biff and bang that they ran for their lives and haven't been heard of since.

# The water tortoise

Jamie had a tortoise named Topsy; she was rather old and her shell was none too shiny, but Jamie loved her just the same.

Jamie often sat and watched as Topsy chomped her way through lettuces and tomatoes with her strange, hard jaws.

One day when Jamie went to feed his pet he found Topsy had gone. She had somehow managed to dig her way out of her pen and had disappeared. Jamie searched all over the garden, and his mum and dad knocked on their neighbours' doors asking if anyone had seen her, but it was no good; Topsy was nowhere to be found. Dad was sure that someone would find her and look after her, but poor Jamie felt miserable.

Winter came and went, and when the weather began to get warmer Jamie noticed that the man in the pet shop had some more tortoises for sale. He would have liked to have one, but Dad and Mum didn't want him to lose another tortoise and get upset again, so they said no. So that was that.

Or so Jamie thought, until one afternoon when he came in from school his mum said, 'Come into the kitchen and shut your eyes, we've got a surprise for you.'

When he opened his eyes, there in front of him was a tortoise with a shiny shell covered with beautiful patterns, and bright black eyes. Strangest of all, it was swimming around in a glass tank full of water.

‘A water tortoise!’ said Jamie. Dad told him it was called a terrapin and spent most of its time in the water or resting on the rock in the middle of the tank.

Next day they went to the library and borrowed a book which explained how to look after the terrapin, how to feed it and keep it warm. Jamie was proud of his water tortoise, and he was very glad to know that it could never run away.

# Dick and Dora

Dick and Dora, the grey and white goose and gander, were very sad. The other birds who lived on the island in the lake would have nothing to do with them.

'Go away,' quacked the ducks, 'this is our feeding place.' Dick and Dora were chased up the bank into the car park, where the ground was hard and sticky. Even when they settled there they had no peace, for nasty smelly motor cars drove in and they made such rude noises with their horns that Dick and Dora had to move again.

'Oh dear,' said Dora. 'How unkind everyone is.'

'Never mind,' said Dick. 'There's a little house over there, and the door is open. Let's look inside.'

So they waddled across the car park, and put their heads through the door. It said 'Library' in large letters over the entrance, but Dick and Dora couldn't read.

Miss Page the librarian was stamping books at the counter when she saw them coming in. 'Off you go. No animals allowed in here,' she cried. Dick and Dora didn't like the sound of her voice so they quickly scuttled off.

Later that day Farmer Brown came into the library. He was worried. 'It's those geese,' he said to Miss Page. 'They are on the main road now. I'm afraid they'll be run over. Do you know who they belong to?'

'No, nobody knows,' said Miss Page.

'Well, I think I'll take them up to the pond on my farm. They can't come to any harm there,' said Farmer Brown.

But when he got back to the road, Dick and Dora had gone. He went to the lake but there was no sign of them. He crossed the road, and was just passing the village school when he heard shrieks of laughter and shouting coming from the playground at the back.

Mrs Timms the teacher came hurrying to the gate. 'Oh, Mr Brown,' she said. 'Perhaps you can help us. There are two geese in the children's paddling pool, and we can't get rid of them.'

'So that's where they are. I've been looking for them,' said Farmer Brown. 'Come along you two, that's quite enough,' he said as the geese splashed and squawked in the shallow pool.

'Just when we were enjoying ourselves,' quacked Dick as they were bundled into the Land Rover and driven away.

But when they reached the farm they had a lovely surprise. 'Why look at this!' they said. 'A big pond all to ourselves. How wonderful! Someone cares about us after all.'

# The little train

The little train that ran from Dunderry to the sea was called the stopping train, because it stopped at every station on the way to let the people out and in again.

'You're a very slow train,' said an express train who was standing next to it in the siding one day. 'I run hundreds of miles without stopping.'

'Yes, I know,' said the little stopping train, 'but I can't do that, because I have to let the people in and out of me.'

'I rush past them all,' boasted the express train. 'I make the platforms shake and the waiting people tremble. I don't notice silly little stations at all.'

After listening to the express train, the little stopping train decided that the next day *he* wouldn't stop at all the stations either. He would take his passengers straight from Dunderry to the sea. Perhaps the people would like it.

The next day the people got on the stopping train, the

luggage was put in too, the guard waved his flag and off they went. 'Chuff chuff,' the little train went. Faster and faster he hurried. He rushed past all the stations blowing his whistle until the people who were waiting for him on the station platforms were nearly deafened.

The people in the train shouted at him to let them get out. The driver shouted at him but the little train went faster and faster, saying to himself, 'I'm an express train for today!'

When he reached the sea, the little stopping train said, 'I enjoyed that but I won't do it again, because I went so fast, I couldn't see the children wave their hands at me. No, I'll never do it again,' and he didn't, either.

# Tara's tomatoes

Tara's mum and dad had given her a little part of the garden for her very own. She made a tiny rockery, with stones, and she grew some flowers from seeds. Tara was especially thrilled when Dad helped her to grow some tomato plants there.

She watched proudly as, during the early summer, her plants gradually grew bigger and bigger. Soon they were almost as tall as Tara herself, and they had plenty of strong green leaves. Tiny green tomatoes began to appear here and there on the plants.

'When they have had plenty of sun, they will grow big and red,' said Mum. 'Then we'll be able to eat them, Tara. Home-grown tomatoes are really delicious, you know.'

Tara was very excited and proud but, although she waited and waited, for weeks and weeks, and the tomatoes did grow a little bigger, they did not turn red.

'I'm afraid it's because we aren't having much sun this summer,' said Dad. 'Your tomatoes just aren't ripening.'

Tara was disappointed to think that her very own tomatoes would be no use, after all.

Then Mum said, 'But they will be useful, Tara. Instead of wasting them, we'll cook them, and make them into green tomato chutney. Chutney is a special pickle – delicious to eat.'

Soon, Tara and her mum were busy picking all the tomatoes from Tara's plants. They washed the tomatoes, and Mum chopped them up into small pieces. They mixed them with chopped apple, vinegar, brown sugar, sultanas, onions and spices. Mum boiled everything together in a big saucepan, and when the mixture was ready, Tara helped her to put it into jars. Mum put lids on the jars, and Tara wrote a label for each jar saying: 'Tara's Green Tomato Chutney'.

Tara and her mum and dad had some of the chutney with their cold meat salad that very evening – and how they enjoyed it!

'You see, Tara, your own tomatoes were useful, after all!' said Mum.

# Michael's garden

Michael liked to help Daddy in the garden. He would dig, and pull up weeds, and Daddy said he didn't know what he'd do without him. One day, Daddy dug a little patch of garden and put a row of stones around it. He said that Michael could have it for his very own.

Next time they went to the shops Mummy said he could choose a packet of seeds to plant in his garden. He looked at all the beautiful pictures on the front of the packets, and chose one labelled 'Pansies' because the flowers looked as if they had faces.

That afternoon Michael took his red spade and dug some holes in his garden. Mum showed him how to put the seeds in and cover them up with earth. She filled the watering can and gave them a long drink.

In the morning, while Mum was toasting the bread for breakfast, Michael went out to look at his garden. When he came in again he was crying.

'Why, whatever's the matter?' said Mummy.

'My garden doesn't work!' sobbed Michael. 'There are no pansies at all.'

Mummy laughed, and told Michael that the seeds needed rain and sunshine before they could grow, and it would take a bit of time.

A few weeks later, when Michael looked at his garden again, he saw some tiny green leaves poking out of the ground. His garden did work after all!

# Elephant

Many, many years ago, the elephant was a most unhappy animal. It was about the time God sent his angel to paint all the animals. The elephant was the last to be painted and as he was so large the angel mixed all the left-over paint together and splashed it over the elephant.

When the paint dried out the elephant's skin was a dull grey colour and it was all wrinkled because he had been painted too quickly. 'Bother,' said the elephant. 'Why should I have a grey wrinkled coat, when my brother leopard has a fine spotted fur coat all gold and brown?'

He decided to cheer himself up with a cool sloshy mud bath, and while he was enjoying this mud bath the thought came to him that he couldn't possibly have a lovely mud bath if he had a fine fur coat. Oh, dear no! The fine fur coat would be ruined.

'I think,' said the elephant, 'my skin is just right for me. I'd only spoil a fur coat,' and he blew mud all over himself happily.

# The peacock

Billy's friend, Karl, was looking very happy. 'Look what I've got,' he said to Billy.

Karl went to his book shelf and he came back with his biggest picture book. There was something peeping from between the pages.

It was a feather! It was the most beautiful feather Billy had ever seen – all blues and greens like a rainbow, all dark and silky with a round coloured spot at the end like a big bird's eye. It was a peacock's feather.

'I keep it on the page where my favourite story is,' said Karl.

'I wish I had a peacock's feather for *my* story-book,' said Billy.

Then, one day Billy's Aunty Babs came for tea and she had a hat on with a feather on it. It was the same as Karl's feather.

'Can I have your peacock's feather to put in my story-book?' said Billy.

'Certainly not!' laughed Aunty Babs. Then she said, 'But if you like peacocks' feathers so much we'll go to the park this afternoon and see the peacock there and we'll ask it to show us its tail.'

So Billy and Aunty Babs walked to the park. Just before they got to the grass where the peacock was, there was a terrible squawking, shrieking noise. 'Peacocks are very noisy birds in spring,' laughed Aunty. Then she pointed to a huge bird with a long drooping tail of feathers that trailed on the floor. The bird was a lovely blue colour with a little feathery crown on its head.

'What a droopy tail,' said Billy. 'Where are all the coloured feathers?'

'Wait and see,' said Aunty.

But nothing happened. So Billy said to the park-keeper, 'Where are the peacock's feathers?' and he told him all about Karl's feather in his picture book.

'Wait and see,' smiled the park-keeper. Then he said, 'Come on, peacock. Show Billy your feathers.'

And suddenly all the peacock's tail feathers rose up in the air into a huge, brilliant-coloured fan. And the peacock strutted round showing off his tail.

The park-keeper picked up something from the grass and gave it to Billy. 'Take it home for your story-book,' he said.

And Billy went home from the park with a peacock's feather of his very own.

# Goalie

Neil's dog liked playing football so much that Neil called him 'Goalie'. Whenever Neil went with his brother to play on the common, or in the field at the back of the flats, Goalie the dog would go with them and run up and down the field trying to get the ball. Until, one day he burst the ball with his sharp teeth!

'That dog is a pest,' said Neil's brother, Andy. 'I wish he would go away and never come back!'

'I don't,' said Neil. 'Goalie is my dog, and he's very clever – aren't you, Goalie?' But when Neil looked round for Goalie – he had gone!

'Don't worry,' said Andy, 'he'll come back as soon as he's hungry.' So they went home for dinner.

'Where's Goalie?' said Dad.

'He'll be here, soon,' said Andy. But Goalie never came. And when Neil and Andy set off for the proper football match in the afternoon Goalie *still* hadn't come back.

Neil was very sad. He kept thinking about Goalie all the time he was watching the match.

But Andy was happy. 'One more goal and we're top of the league!' he said. And the crowd kept shouting, 'Give us a goal . . . Give us a goal.'

Then Neil saw something. It was a brown and white dog with big floppy ears, and it ran right into the middle of the football match and started chasing the ball. It was Goalie!

So the referee blew his whistle and stopped the game. But Goalie didn't stop. He pushed the ball into the net with his nose. And everyone stood up and shouted 'Goal'. Then Goalie ran off the field before anyone could catch him.

The referee started the match again and soon after that Neil and Andy's team scored a *real* goal and won the match.

Then a voice on the loudspeaker said, 'Please come to the manager's office if you've lost a brown and white dog.'

When Neil and Andy got there they found Goalie – wagging his tail! And with him was the *real* goalkeeper!

So Neil told him all about Goalie bursting their football and running off.

Guess what the football team did? They gave Goalie a ball of his very own, and signed it with their names.

# The magic box

Mr Perkins kept the little shop on the corner of the street where Peter lived.

Peter loved Mr Perkin's shop for he sold all the things that children like – sweets, ices, toys and lovely drinks.

On the top shelf was a beautiful red box with gold stripes. 'Mr Perkins,' said Peter one day, 'what do you keep in that box?'

'Ah,' said Mr Perkins, 'there's magic up there. Perhaps I'll let you look inside one day.'

The next day, Patch the puppy pulled Peter's teddy out of his toy cupboard and played very roughly with him.

Poor teddy, one leg was off, and his ears were all chewed up. 'Oh Mummy, my dear teddy. Look at him!' Peter said.

'Don't cry,' said Mummy, 'I have an idea. We'll go and see Mr Perkins and take teddy with us.'

Mr Perkins looked at poor teddy and took down his magic box. Inside there was new arms, legs, eyes, heads and even cloth for mending torn teddy bears and broken dolls.

'So that's what you keep in your magic box,' said Peter.

'Yes, I'll certainly have to work some magic on your teddy. You leave him here and he'll soon be as good as new.'

# Squirrel

Squirrel was busy. He scampered here and there, eagerly hunting for beech nuts and acorns to store for the winter.

He knew that, when winter comes, the world is a very harsh place for small animals who have not provided for themselves during the autumn.

Alan was out walking in the woods when he saw the squirrel coming towards him. Squirrel knew immediately that here was a friend.

He scampered across the green turf towards Alan and stood up on his two hind legs, and held up his two front paws as if to say, 'Please help me.'

Well, just as the squirrel knew that Alan was a friend, so Alan knew that the squirrel was telling him that winter was coming and he had not gathered up nearly enough nuts to last him through the hard, cold season. It was plain to Alan that Squirrel was asking, 'Please help me to find more nuts.'

So, while the squirrel hunted in one direction, Alan hunted in another and he soon found a heap of the very best beech nuts underneath a tall beech tree. Alan gathered them together and gave them to the squirrel who carried them away one by one and buried them.

When he had hidden them all, he came and chattered his thanks to Alan, who nodded and then went on his way.

# The monkeys

Ajit lived in a very hot sunny place where there are monkeys. Ajit's mum and dad made hats. They made lots and lots of straw hats to keep the sun off people's heads.

One day Dad said to Ajit, 'You must take all our straw hats to the market to sell.' So Ajit took two big baskets of straw hats and fastened them to his little donkey, Dodo, and set off to market. But it was very hot and it was a long way. Ajit began to feel tired and his legs began to ache.
Worst of all, he had forgotten to put his very own hat on.

'I wish I had put my hat on,' he said. So he sat down under a shady tree to rest. But there was something Ajit didn't know. He didn't know that the tree was full of cheeky monkeys! They were all sitting amongst the leaves watching him.

Then Ajit had an idea. He took one of the hats out of the baskets and put it on. Then he fell fast asleep.

When he woke up he had a terrible shock! The hat baskets were all empty! 'Where have all the other hats gone?' he cried. Although he hunted everywhere there wasn't a hat to be seen. Someone had stolen them.

'What shall we do, Dodo?' he said to his donkey. At first, Dodo just blinked, then she shook her head and jerked it up towards the tree. Ajit looked up and saw something strange. It was a monkey sitting amongst the branches – and it had a straw hat on! As he looked more closely he saw more and more monkeys – all wearing *his* hats!

'MY STRAW HATS,' he gasped. 'But how shall I get them back? Those monkeys must have seen me putting on a hat before I went to sleep, and they have copied me!'

He had an idea. He stood under the tree and he took off his own hat and threw it on the floor. Then he waited.

And very soon the monkeys all began to take their hats off and throw them on the floor. Until it was raining hats from the tree!

'They have copied me again,' laughed Ajit. Then he picked up all his straw hats and put them back in the baskets.

'Aren't monkeys funny?' he said to Dodo. And when he got to market he told everyone about the funny monkeys.

# The little clock

Every night at eight o'clock the little clock that stood on the shelf by the window stopped ticking. Nothing and nobody could make it go. Father shook it and Mother tried hard to wind it a little bit more but it was all no use. The little clock refused to go.

Every morning when the grandfather clock in the hall chimed eight, the little clock began to tick again and he went on all through the day until eight o'clock at night came round again.

No-one could understand it, no-one at all, not even the little mouse that ran up and down the grandfather clock. 'Little clock,' said the tiny mouse, 'why do you stop ticking at night?'

'Because night is the time for sleeping. It's lonely here ticking when everyone is sleeping,' the little clock said.

'Grandfather Clock keeps on ticking all night long,' argued the little mouse, 'and he's a great deal older than you.'

'Maybe, but he has you for company,' the little clock said sadly.

'Mm, yes,' agreed the mouse, 'and we have lots of fun together. I go up and down, and down and up him every night until he strikes one and sends me away.'

'Where do you go to then?' asked the little clock.

'Why, back to my hole under the floorboards,' said the mouse.

The little clock was silent for a while and then he said coaxingly, 'If I decided to stay awake just for once perhaps, would you come and play with me after the grandfather clock strikes one?'

'Yes, of course I would. I'll come tonight,' said the mouse.

The little clock could hardly wait for one o'clock to come round. He ticked loudly and quickly all throughout the day until Mother and Father were worried about him.

At last the grandfather clock struck one and the time came for the little mouse to join the little clock. And forever after that the mouse came after one o'clock struck and kept the little clock happy and ticking away all night long.

# Disappearing Daisy

Dina's doll kept disappearing. 'My doll's gone again,' she said to Mum. 'I put it in my doll's pram. But now there's only Teddy left. Where can it have gone?'

'I haven't seen your doll,' said Mum. 'Are you sure you put it in your doll's pram? It couldn't have gone on its own.'

So Dina went to look for Daisy. She looked in her toy-cupboard. She looked in her bed, and she looked outside.

She even asked the postman because the postman delivered all the letters to the flats and talked to everyone.

'What was she wearing?' asked the postman.

'A long white night-dress,' said Dina. 'She hasn't got any other clothes.'

'I'll keep a look out,' smiled the postman. And away he went.

But when Dina got back to her doll's pram again, *Daisy was there*, sitting next to Teddy.

Then the next day it happened again. Daisy went again. 'Do you think she can walk or fly, Mum?' said Dina.

'No,' laughed Mum, 'but it really is a puzzle. We shall just have to watch her very carefully.'

Then Dina had an idea. She took Daisy out of the doll's pram and sat her right in the middle of the kitchen table. 'We'll leave her there, Mum, where we can see her all the time.'

But when Dina and Mum went out of the kitchen, Daisy disappeared *again*.

At tea-time Dina told her gran, who lived with them, all about Daisy disappearing.

Then Gran laughed and said, 'Don't worry – she won't be disappearing any more. Go to my bedroom and look on my bed.'

And there – on Gran's bed – was Daisy. But she wasn't in a white nightie any more. She had all proper clothes on – a pretty blue dress and a knitted pram set with a blue bonnet and blue woolly leggings. She looked beautiful.

'I wanted to give you a nice surprise,' smiled Gran. 'I had to keep taking Daisy away to fit the clothes properly. But now I've finished them!'

# The present

One day, Mrs Green met John at the shops. 'Would anyone in your house like a goldfish?' she said. 'We're going to Australia, and it's rather a long way for Guinea – our goldfish – to go. If you fetch a jam-jar round to our house, I'll give him to you.'

'I'll give Dad that goldfish as a surprise present,' said John, 'because he always takes me to see the fish in the park.' So he ran home for a jam-jar. But there was only one jam-jar in the house. One very large one – full of strawberry jam.

'I shall just have to eat up the jam very quickly so as to empty the jar for the goldfish,' said John. So he said, 'Please Mum – make me lots of bread and jam for my dinner.'

When John had finished he was nearly bursting. 'I must have eaten a *ton* of jam,' he said. But when he looked at the big jam-jar there was still lots left. 'I'll never get through all that,' he gasped.

Mum went to the kitchen to do some baking. 'You can help me to make some jam tarts,' she said.

John was very pleased and he puts lots of jam in the tarts to get the jar empty. But *still* there was a bit left.

Then Mum gave him a bit of pastry and said, 'Make what you like.' And he made *another* big jam tart and emptied the jar.

John took the big clean jar to Mrs Green's for Guinea the goldfish. It was just the right size. So he put a pretty label on and wrote: 'To Dad From John'.

Dad was so pleased that he took John to the shops and bought Guinea a proper fish tank to swim in. So John made *another* present. He stuck pretty coloured paper on the empty jar and gave it to Mum for flowers.

# Andrew

Andrew liked water. He liked splashing in the bath, sailing his boat on the pond, and playing beside the sea. But he didn't like the swimming-pool where his father sometimes took him on Saturdays.

Then his father brought home some bright red arm-bands, the kind that help you to float in water, and a ring that floated too.

When they went to the swimming-pool that Saturday, Andrew put the arm-bands on and, clutching the ring, let his father lead him slowly down the steps into the shallow end.

'Now, try lifting you feet off the bottom,' his father said.

Andrew was afraid, but he slowly lifted first one foot, then the other, off the bottom. He didn't sink.

His father held him up for a while, and then said, 'I'm going to let go now. Don't worry – I shan't let you sink.'

He let go of Andrew, who clung to the floating ring. Suddenly, Andrew realised that he was floating, on his own. He smiled, and kicked a bit with his feet, and he and the ring moved along in the water.

It was a nice feeling. He decided there was nothing to be afraid of, after all.

# Caroline's rainbow

Caroline lay in bed and listened to the story her mummy was reading.

'And they found the pot of gold at the end of the rainbow,' said her mummy. Then she smiled and closed the book.

'I wish *I* could find the end of a rainbow,' said Caroline sleepily.

Next morning it was raining. 'I won't see a rainbow today,' Caroline said sadly. But after dinner, the sun came out and she played in the garden.

A bird sang sweetly overhead. Caroline looked up. She stared in surprise. Across the sky was a beautiful rainbow!

Caroline smiled with delight. 'It's red, orange, yellow, green, blue and purple!' she said. 'I *must* see what is at the end of *my* rainbow!'

She ran towards the rainbow, but, as she ran, the pretty colours faded away. 'I shall never see what is at the end of my rainbow *now*!' she sighed.

Then she smiled. Just where the rainbow had touched the ground was a patch of beautiful wild flowers. Caroline picked them eagerly, and hurried home.

Her mummy stared at the red, orange, yellow, green, blue and purple flowers.

'I found them at the end of my rainbow!' smiled Caroline.

# A special prize

Janet decided that when she grew up she would be a jockey because she loved horses and ponies. She hadn't any of her own but Uncle Jack kept a pony specially for her on his farm.

Janet loved Snowball very much and every day after school she took some sugar lumps or carrots and went to feed her.

On Saturday mornings, Janet went up to Uncle Jack's very early, because he let her groom Snowball each week on Saturday. She stood on an upturned box and carefully brushed the pony until her coat was as smooth as silk.

'Janet,' said Uncle Jack one day, 'there's a pony show being held in the village next week. How about entering Snowball? There is a prize for the best kept pony and you certainly look after Snowball well.'

'What's the prize going to be?' asked Janet.

'I think it's a day at the races,' replied Uncle Jack. 'Now wouldn't you love to win that?'

'Oh, yes, I would. What must I do to enter the show?' Janet said.

'I have a form which I will help you to fill in, but you had better ask Mummy and Daddy first,' said Uncle Jack.

Her mummy and daddy agreed that it was a lovely idea and Janet could hardly wait until the show day arrived. She spent all the week before grooming Snowball and Mummy gave her some brightly coloured streamers to hang from the pony's reins.

There were lots of ponies on show and the owners stood by nervously, waiting for the lady judge. She looked carefully at each pony and felt them all over. Janet held tightly on to Snowball waiting for their turn. The kind lady came at last and said, 'My, you have got a beauty there. I can see she has been very well cared for.'

Mummy, Daddy and Uncle Jack clapped loudly. 'Well done,' they told Janet as the judge fastened a big red rosette on to Snowball.

Janet, Mummy, Daddy and Uncle Jack spent a wonderful day at the races and Janet was even more certain that one day she would be a jockey.

# Chapatis

Yasmine was excited because it was baking day at the playschool and her mummy was coming to help.

'Children,' said the playschool lady, 'we are going to make some chapatis this morning. Yasmine's mummy, Mrs Hasnie, is going to show us how.'

Mrs Hasnie and Yasmine opened a shopping bag and took out a large tin box, a big baking bowl, some salt, a sieve, a packet of flour and some wooden spoons.

Next Yasmine opened the tin and proudly showed her little friends the lovely round chapatis.

'They are a bit like pancakes,' the children said.

'Yes, they are,' answered Yasmine, 'but we don't put lemon juice and sugar on them.'

'We must first sieve the flour so there won't be lumps in our chapatis,' said Mrs Hasnie.

'Now the salt goes in,' Yasmine's mummy told them, 'but just a pinch or the chapatis will be too salty.'

Yasmine made a big hole in the middle of the flour and added a little cold water, then she stirred hard with a big wooden spoon.

All the children took turns at beating the mixture whilst Yasmine put in the rest of the water.

Soon they had made a smooth batter, free of lumps.

'Good,' said Mrs Hasnie and she asked the playschool lady to heat up the frying pan.

When the pan was really hot, Yasmine's mummy put a spoonful of batter into it and spread it out into a round shape with a wooden spatula.

When the chapatis were cooked on one side, Mrs Hasnie carefully turned them over and waited until they were a golden brown colour on both sides.

'Can we eat them at milk time?' the children asked.

'That's a good idea, but what shall we put on them?' asked the playschool lady.

'We have brought some golden syrup today, but we have different things with chapatis when we eat them for lunch,' said Mrs Hasnie.

'Yes,' Yasmine told the children, 'sometimes we have curried chicken or fish.'

The children each made their own chapati but the grown-ups helped in case they burned themselves or the chapatis!

# The pigeon race

At the bottom of Jackie and Kim's garden, there was a pigeon loft where their dad kept racing pigeons. (Pigeon lofts are special little wooden houses for pigeons.)

One day Jackie and Kim had a big surprise. Their dad gave them two pigeons. 'These two aren't very good at racing,' said Dad, 'but they'll make nice pets. So if you look after them properly – you can have them.'

The pigeons were called Popsy and Mopsy and they had pearly grey and white feathers.

'Fancy Dad saying Popsy and Mopsy aren't good at racing,' said Jackie. 'Let's have a race with them and see. We'll take them to the park in the big shopping basket. Then, we'll let them fly home on their own and we'll ask Mum to let us know which one gets back first.'

So Jackie and Kim took the pigeons to the park. They went right to the middle of a big stretch of grass, and they let Popsy and Mopsy out of the basket. But guess what those two pigeons did?

First they went flying round in circles as if they were playing aeroplanes. Then they went flipping about over the tops of all the trees.

Then they flew close to the pond in the park and landed on the grass right next to where a little girl was feeding some baby ducklings. The two pigeons managed to eat quite a lot of the ducklings' bread, but before Jackie and Kim could creep up and catch them, they flew up into the air again.

'Perhaps they think the park aviary is a pigeon loft!' said Jackie, as they watched the pigeons walking about on the aviary roof.

'We'll just have to go back home and see if they come back to their loft later on. They don't seem to like racing at all,' said Kim.

When they got back, Dad was down the garden with his proper racing pigeons.

'How are Popsy and Mopsy getting on?' he asked.

'They've got lost in the park,' said Kim. 'I hope someone will see the little rings they are wearing round their ankles and send them back to us.'

Then Mum called from the house. 'Hurry up, tea's ready. I thought you two had got lost in the park.'

'It's Popsy and Mopsy that have got lost, Mum,' said Jackie.

'Popsy and Mopsy?' said Mum. 'They're not lost! They got back ages ago. They're up there on the roof – near the chimney-pot.'

'They must be better at racing than we thought!' said Jackie and Kim.

# A little nut tree

Roger was watching television. They were singing songs on the programme he was watching, and one of the songs went like this:

> 'I had a little nut tree
> And nothing would it bear
> But a silver nut-meg
> And a golden pear.'

'Have we any silver nut-megs or golden pears, Mum?' said Roger.

'We've got a nut-meg,' laughed Mum, 'but it isn't a silver one. It's small and brown like a little nut.'

'Have we got a golden pear, then?' said Roger.

'No,' said Mum, 'But Mrs Brown next door has a pear tree in the garden.'

'Does it have golden pears on it?' asked Roger.

'If the pears are left on the tree until autumn,' said Mum, 'they get ripe, and they turn a beautiful golden shade.'

And sure enough – when autumn came the pears on Mrs Brown's pear tree went all golden.

Roger found some silver paper off a chocolate bar and he asked Mum for her nut-meg. Then he covered the little brown nut in silver paper.

'It's a silver nut-meg, now!' he said, and he took it round to Mrs Brown's house.

'Please can I have one of your golden pears, to go with my silver nut-meg, Mrs Brown?' he asked.

'Of course you can, Roger,' said Mrs Brown.

'Now I've a silver nut-meg *and* a golden pear,' he laughed.

# The new curtains

Jenny was ill. She lay in bed and stared at her curtains. They were old and worn and drab, and flapped wearily against the window. Jenny found them dull to look at but was too ill to sit up and read.

Mummy came in and looked at Jenny anxiously. She saw her staring at the dowdy curtains and had an idea. 'I'll go out right away Jenny, and buy a length of pretty material and make you some bright new curtains to look at.'

Mummy worked hard, and by tea-time the curtains were finished and hung up. All that week Jenny lay quietly, watching the pictures on her new curtains.

The curtains were green and blue and had flowers and animals and birds in orange, red and yellow. There were tall reeds to one side and a flock of geese flying over a cool blue lake. They were so nice that she was sure they helped her to get better.

# Lemon-curd

Richard loved lemon-curd. He liked its nice bright colour and he liked its taste. He ate it for breakfast *and* tea *and* supper every day.

One day, he had just finished his breakfast when Mum said, 'We're going to visit Mrs Smurthwaite this morning.'

'Who's Mrs Smurthwaite?' Richard wanted to know.

'She's an old lady and she hasn't been very well, so we're going to cheer her up,' his mother said.

Richard didn't think that sounded exciting at all. 'I'd rather play with my cars,' he said.

'You can choose a car to take with you,' said Mum. So Richard chose his green car that went by itself when it had been wound up.

The old lady lived in a funny little cottage. Mum tapped at the door and Mrs Smurthwaite called, 'Come in – the door isn't locked.' She was sitting in a big chair by the fire with a rug wrapped round her knees.

Richard thought she looked *very* old. There was a ginger cat lying beside her. Richard stroked its soft fur and it purred loudly. 'Prrrrrr!'

'What a lovely car you've got there,' said Mrs Smurthwaite.

'It goes by itself,' said Richard. 'Look, I'll show you.'

He wound up the car with the little key and then put it on the floor. 'Rrrrrrrr' went the car as it raced across the room, 'Rrrrrrrrrrrrrr'.

The big ginger cat sat up and watched the car. Then she chased it under the table and stopped it with her paw.

'Ginger thinks it's a mouse,' said Mrs Smurthwaite.

Then Mum asked if Richard could play in the garden and the old lady said of course he could, so Richard went outside. When he looked around the garden at the back of the cottage he couldn't believe his eyes! There, at either side of the path and under the apple tree were masses of lovely flowers exactly the same colour as lemon-curd. He went running back into the house.

'Mum,' he said, 'Mrs Smurthwaite's got lots of lemon-curd flowers in her garden.' His mother and the old lady laughed.

'They are yellow pansies,' Mum said.

'They're my favourite flowers,' said Richard. 'Can we have some in our garden?'

Then Mrs Smurthwaite said she would give him some plants to take home to start a little garden of his very own. Richard was pleased!

He went outside again and wound up his green car. 'Rrrrrrrr' it said as it buzzed its way down the path. Ginger came to join the game, too. What a lovely morning they had!

# Green apples

All the trees in Mr Plumley's orchard had lots of apples.

'It's a very good year for fruit!' said Mr Plumley happily to himself, as he gathered his crop.

The apple trees were very happy to know that Mr and Mrs Plumley were so pleased with their fruit. Only one tree was sad. She had waited and waited, but Mr Plumley never picked her apples, and she couldn't understand why.

'My apples are big – almost the biggest of all the apples in the orchard,' sighed the sad apple tree. 'Maybe it is because my apples are green, and not red as most of the other apples are. I don't know why my apples haven't turned red. They have had just as much sun as all the other trees. I simply don't understand it all.'

The tree became so sad and droopy that it began to lose its leaves before all the other trees.

Then, one day, right at the end of October, when Mr and Mrs Plumley came into the orchard they came right up to the sad apple tree!

‘It’s my turn!’ thought the sad apple tree. ‘It’s my turn at last. Mr and Mrs Plumley haven’t forgotten about my apples, after all. Now I must listen to what they are saying.’

Mr Plumley said to his wife, ‘We’ll keep these apples for ourselves. We won’t send them to market.’

‘Quite right, my dear,’ said Mrs Plumley. ‘After all, this tree is our only cooking-apple tree.’

‘Cooking apples!’ said the apple tree to itself. ‘So I’m a cooking-apple tree, am I? That’s why my apples are so green. They are *meant* to be green.’

How happy the cooking-apple tree was then! She didn’t mind about losing her leaves, or about the long winter months ahead. Now she could look forward to next spring when her blossom would appear. After that, she knew her apples would start growing again – her lovely green cooking apples. The cooking-apple tree felt so proud and – never again was she known as a sad apple tree!

# A special day

Just before Christmas, when a thin sprinkling of snow covered the garden, Adam and Penny looked out of the window at the brown sparrows. The sparrows were quarrelling over the scraps Mummy had put on the lawn.

In the kitchen Mummy was busy making mince pies. Adam and Penny decided to help. As they rolled and patted and cut and cooked, Adam asked, 'Mummy, do sparrows know about Christmas?'

Mummy said she didn't think so, and the children said that they wished they could include the sparrows in all their Christmas fun.

Mummy thought, and then she said, 'There is something you could do for the sparrows on Christmas morning.'

Adam and Penny woke up extra early on Christmas Day. Mum got an old branch from the garden and stuck it in a bucket of sand, and Penny and Adam began to thread all kinds of things that sparrows like on to pieces of red wool.

They used currants and apples, peanuts and bacon rinds, and when they'd finished they tied the streamers on to the branch and stood the bucket in the middle of the lawn.

Sparrows came from everywhere and sat on the branch, pulling and pecking. 'Well,' said Mummy, 'I don't know if they understand about Christmas, but you've certainly made it a very special day for the sparrows.'

# Uncle Jeremy's wig

'Please don't keep looking at it!' Aunt Beth told her nieces Emma and Lucy when they first saw Uncle Jeremy's wig.

'He only wears it for paying visits,' she continued, 'and for going to work. All the rest of the time it sits there on the dresser.'

The girls giggled and ran off. 'I'd love to try Uncle's wig on, wouldn't you?' said Emma. 'Bet I'd look a sight!'

Very quietly they crept back into the living room. Uncle Jeremy was having his afternoon nap in the armchair and Aunt Beth was busy painting the garden fence.

'NOW!' commanded Emma, 'Quick!' Lucy leapt forward, snatched up the wig and they ran upstairs.

They played for hours with the wig, pulling it this way and that, and pretending to be Uncle Jeremy. So busy were they enjoying themselves that they didn't notice that the wig was coming to pieces, until only a little black tuft was left.

'We can't put *that* back on the dresser,' wailed Emma, 'oh, what have we done?'

All they could do was to offer Uncle Jeremy locks of their own hair to have another wig made.

Now people often comment about Uncle Jeremy's *superb* hair!

# The snow picnic

Colin and Kate looked out of the kitchen window. It was a lovely crisp October morning. The hills were ablaze with autumn colour. Trees sparkled copper gold in the sunshine and the leaves made a lovely crunching sound as the wind blew them about.

'Can we go out, Mummy?' asked Colin.

'Yes dear. But wrap up warmly. It's quite chilly this morning.'

'May we take something to eat?' said Kate, looking at a pile of freshly baked cakes.

'What a good idea,' said Colin. 'We can have a picnic!'

'A picnic in October?' laughed Mummy. But she gathered together some of the cakes, and put them in a bag with two apples, some chocolate and a bottle of lemonade.

Colin and Kate set out across the field. They stopped to say hello to the farmer's cows, then jumped over the stile at the bottom of the field, and climbed up the steep hill.

Their favourite place was right at the top of the hill. It was a large oak tree with a hollow trunk. They climbed inside and munched happily on the chocolate bars. Kate had brought a card game, so they played two games of 'snap'.

Kate pulled her woolly hat further over her ears. 'Gosh, it's turning cold,' she shivered.

'Let's play outside,' said Colin. 'We will soon get warm.'

They jumped out of the tree. But instead of falling on a bed of leaves, they found the ground blanketed with cold white snow.

'Snow?' said Kate. 'Snow!' shouted Colin. 'What a surprise!' He gathered a handful and threw it at Kate. She laughed and threw one back. They had a wonderful time in the snow, running and jumping and rolling about. They made a snowman and a snow house, and then decided to have their picnic.

'A snow picnic!' laughed Kate.

'Yum,' said Colin, his mouth full of cake. They sat on the big curling roots of the oak tree and ate the cakes and apples. Snowflakes fell gently all around them. Kate tried to count them, but there were far too many. They finished off the chocolate and washed it down with lemonade.

'That was the best picnic I have ever had,' said Kate, and Colin agreed.

# The jungle

The jungle was troubled. In every tree the monkeys chattered angrily, swaying from branch to branch. The green parrots squawked and flapped their wings, and on the ground the armour-plated armadillo and slinky lizard whisked nervously about.

The giant gorilla had overheard that their jungle was to be cut down and turned into a cocoa plantation.

The orange and black stripy tiger, who was lord of all the jungle creatures, paced up and down in the clearing. The hot jungle sun shone on to his stripes. His ferocious eyes gleamed with anger. He had to find a way to save the jungle.

Suddenly the stripy tiger lashed his tail, and, lifting his head high into the air, roared loudly into the night. All the jungle creatures heard the noise and knew he had decided what to do. One by one they crept to the clearing until they were gathered in a circle around the stripy tiger.

'I have thought of a plan,' he proudly announced. 'I have decided to scare the men when they come with their tree-cutting-down machines and their earth-moving

machines. We will frighten them away. Go home now and, until they arrive, I want you to practise being fierce and cruel and terrible.'

The animals rushed away back to their dens and lairs and nests and holes, and they practised so hard being fierce and roared and howled so loudly that they frightened one another.

On the day the jungle was to be cut down the giant gorilla, who was on the look-out, heard a noise on the horizon and saw the machines approaching. Quickly he clambered back through the trees to warn the stripy tiger. 'Call the alarm, stripy tiger. They're coming.'

The lord of the jungle raised his head and roared, and all the jungle creatures heard the sign and ran to their posts.

When the men arrived with their machines, they saw between every tree a long line of fearsome jungle creatures standing resolute and brave. The stripy tiger gave his roar, and all together the creatures roared and grunted, howled and squeaked. Then they started to advance.

'This jungle is no ordinary jungle,' one of the men said, his eyes wide with fear. 'It is full of the most terrible beasts I have ever known. I'm not going a step further.'

As the jungle creatures advanced, the men backed away, then jumped into their machines and drove off at top speed. They said they would never go near the jungle again.

# The baby goldfish

Luke lived in the middle of a great big city, but he was luckier than a lot of his friends, for his house had a garden and, best of all, in the garden was a fishpond which had at least ten goldfish in it.

Luke fed the goldfish every Saturday with some food he bought from Mrs Salmon's pet shop.

'Now, only feed them once a week, Luke,' Mrs Salmon had told him. 'The rest of the time they can eat the insects that float on the surface of the water. Goldfish are nearly always hungry and will eat everything you give them, and fat goldfish aren't healthy.'

Every Saturday, the goldfish were waiting for Luke. It was almost as if they counted off the days of the week on their fins, Luke thought to himself with a smile. They hovered near the surface with their mouths open, while Luke sprinkled the food about like pepper.

They were very greedy goldfish and, with a few large gulps, all the food was gone!

One late spring day, Luke was cleaning out some paper which had blown into the pond when he noticed a very tiny dark fish swimming under a water lily. He looked more closely at the water and saw that there was not one but at least twenty little fish swimming around. He couldn't understand how they had got there.

He ran in to ask his mum but she couldn't understand it either. So they looked up 'goldfish' in a big book and discovered that baby goldfish often had dark scales when they were young, but would gradually become gold as they got older.

Luke was thrilled to know they had baby goldfish, and every day he would examine the little fish to see if they were changing colour. At first nothing happened, but as the months passed, the little fish began to grow and change. They became silvery, and then yellowy, and then a pale, sunshiny gold just like their parents.

But Luke saw that two of the babies never did quite manage to become completely gold – they remained silvery with a few gold scales and were very pretty and less shy than the others and would often come to the surface of the water and blink at him. They were his favourites and he always gave them just a little bit extra to eat.

# The parcel

Sarah and Ben were playing in the garden one summer day, but they were hot and cross and kept quarrelling.

Ben snatched Sarah's doll out of its pram and pretended to throw it over the hedge. Sarah didn't like being teased and rode away on Ben's bike. Then their Uncle John came into the garden.

'Hello,' he said, 'I've brought you two a present as it's such a hot day.'

Ben and Sarah stopped looking cross and looked at Uncle John instead. He handed them a small, flat parcel.

'It's not very big,' he said, 'but give it air and water and it will grow into something lovely for you.'

The children were puzzled. 'The parcel is flat – it must be a book,' said Ben.

'I think it's a plant – they need air and water,' said Sarah.

The children unwrapped the parcel, and there was a lovely brightly coloured paddling pool waiting to be unfolded and blown up.

Sarah gave Ben his bike back so that they could blow up the paddling pool with the pump, and then she ran to find the garden hose.

Uncle John helped the children to fill the pool with water and they had a great time splashing and paddling.

# The sugar mouse

Pinky was a sugar mouse who lived on a tray in a grocer's shop, amongst the biscuits and bread and currants.

All the other sugar mice on the tray teased Pinky. They were snowy white with tidy tails, but Pinky was pink because the factory had made him that way by mistake. Also, his tail was too long and nobody had ever wanted to buy him. The children always looked at him and laughed and then bought a neat, tidy white mouse instead.

But one day a little girl called Samantha came into the shop and asked for a sugar mouse.

'Have you got any pink ones?' asked Samantha, which made Pinky feel quivery and excited.

'Well, only this one,' said the grocer, waving Pinky gently from side to side by his tail.

Samantha clapped her hands in delight. 'Aren't you sweet?' she said to Pinky. 'You're much too sweet to eat, but I might give you a little lick now and then!'

# Autumn

Robin sat at the window and watched the autumn leaves falling to the ground. They sailed softly and landed lightly on the earth like feathers falling from a bird. They made a brightly-coloured carpet on the ground of red and orange and yellow.

'Why do the leaves fall from the trees in autumn, Mummy?' he asked as she prepared tea.

'They are old and worn out by the end of the year, Robin. The tree gets tired of growing and settles down for a winter's rest.'

'When do the new leaves come again? I wish they would hurry. The branches look so cold and bare without them,' said Robin.

'It won't be very long, you'll see,' said Mummy smiling. 'In Spring the fresh green leaves uncurl from buds and grow all over again.'

Just then Daddy came home from work, and after tea he said to Robin, 'Come and help me clear the leaves and make them into a pile. It's November the fifth this Sunday, Guy Fawkes Day, and we must make our bonfire.'

They put on their gumboots and waded through the crunchy leaves sweeping them into a pile. Then Robin collected sticks while Daddy sawed some dead branches off the tree and cut them into logs. Soon they had built a lovely bonfire.

Then Mummy had an idea. 'Let's use your old summer school uniform to make a guy. It's worn at the elbows, and you've outgrown the trousers.'

Carefully they stuffed the shirt and trousers with paper and drew a face on a paper bag filled with straw to make the head. Daddy's old gardening hat was put on the top. It looked grand.

When Sunday came Robin watched the guy burning on the fire. It was strange to see his old uniform blazing away. He turned and said to Mummy, 'My uniform is just like the autumn leaves: worn out and old. When the tree gets its new leaves in spring, couldn't I have a new summer uniform as well?'

'Yes, of course,' said Mummy laughing, 'It won't be long to wait, either. You'll see.'

# The little lamb

One cold morning at the end of the winter a little lamb was born. It greeted the world with a cry, 'Baaaaaaaa'.

It was a very small lamb and very weak. It found it difficult to stand up on its thin little legs so it just lay in the snow at the edge of the field.

Luckily, soon afterwards, Mr Walker the sheep farmer came along with his dog Gyp. Gyp was a very clever dog and he found the little lamb at once.

'Poor little chap,' said Mr Walker picking up the lamb. 'We'd better take you home.'

When they arrived back at the farmhouse, Judith and Ann, Mr Walker's two little girls, were just finishing breakfast.

'Ohhhh!' they said when they saw the little lamb. They nursed it by the fire while their mother warmed some milk. She put the milk in an old feeding bottle that had been Ann's when she was a baby. Then Judith and Ann took it in turns to feed the lamb.

'We'll keep it here until it gets stronger,' their father said.

The girls *were* pleased with their new pet.